Will Acting Spoil Marilyn Monroe?

will acting spoil Marilyn Monroe ?

PETE MARTIN

Doubleday & Company, Inc.
Garden City, New York, 1956

Library of Congress Catalog Card Number: 56-10769

Will Acting Spoil Marilyn Monroe?

I said to Marilyn Monroe

"I've never seen a picture of you with your mouth fully closed or your eyes really wide open. Did some photographer sell you on the idea that having your picture taken that way makes you look sexier?"

She replied in what I'd come to recognize as pure Monroeese.

"The formation of my lids must make them look heavy or else I'm thinking of something," Marilyn told me. "Sometimes I'm thinking of men; other times I'm thinking of some man in particular. It's easier to look sexy when you're thinking of some man in particular. As for my mouth being open all the time, I even sleep with it open. I know, because it's open when I wake up. I never consciously think of my mouth, but I do consciously think about what I'm thinking about."

Tucked away in that paragraph like blueberries in a hot muffin were several genuine Monroeisms. I had studied the subject long enough to be able to tell a genuine Monroeism from a spurious one. Why not? There are people who can sense a real Sam Goldwynism from the synthetic variety.

For example, when I asked her, "Has anyone ever accused you of wearing falsies?" she came through with a genuine Monroeism.

Her greenish-blue eyes flashed indignantly as she told me, "Yes."

"Naturally," she went on, "it was another actress who accused me. My answer to that is, quote: Those who know me better know better. That's all. Unquote."

Another Monroeism followed hard on the heels of that. I said, "I heard that you wowed the marines in Korea when you climbed up onto a platform to say a few words and they whistled at you and made wolf calls."

"I know the time you're talking about," she told me, "and it wasn't in Korea at all; it was at Camp Pendleton, California. They wanted me to say a few words, so I said, 'You fellows down there are always whistling at sweater girls. Well, take away their sweaters and what have you got?' For some reason it seemed to kill them. They screamed and yelled."

Another example came forth when Marilyn was asked if she and a playwright, were having an affair. "How can they say we're having a romance?" she replied reproachfully. "He's married."

Listening to her now, as she talked to me, I thought, *Nobody can write dialogue for her which could possibly sound half as much like her as the dialogue she thinks up for herself.*

Nunnally Johnson, who produced the film, *How to Marry a Millionaire* — it costarred Marilyn — had told me, "When I talked to her when she first came on the lot, I felt as if I were talking to a girl under water. I couldn't tell whether I was getting through to her or not. She lived behind a fuzz curtain."

Johnson also directed *How to Be Very, Very Popular.* When Sheree North took Marilyn's place in that film, he issued an announcement: "Sheree," he said, "will *not* use

8

the Monroe technique in *How to Be Very, Very Popular.* She will play the entire role with her mouth closed."

Marilyn's last sentence to me: "I never consciously think of my mouth, but I do consciously think about what I'm thinking about" seemed a trifle murky, but I didn't have time to work on it, for, without pausing, she said, "Another writer asked me, 'What do you think of sex?' and I told him, 'It's a part of nature. I go along with nature.' Zsa Zsa Gabor was supposed to write an article for a magazine on the subject: What's Wrong with American Men, and I did marginal notes for it. The editor cut out my best lines. I wrote, 'If there's anything wrong with the way American men look at sex, it's not their fault. After all, they're descended from Puritans, who got off the boat on the wrong foot — or was it the Pilgrims? There's still a lot of that puritanical stuff around.' The editor didn't use that one."

Every word she said to me I wrote carefully in a notebook. She told me that she'd rather I wouldn't use a tape-recording machine while interviewing her. "It would make me nervous to see that thing going round and round," she insisted.

So I used pencils and a notebook instead.

But I didn't use them right away.

I had to wait for her to walk from her bedroom into the living room of her apartment, where I was ready to talk to her. It took her an hour and a half to make that journey. At 3:45, Lois Weber, the pleasant young woman who handled the New York Monroe publicity, admitted me to the apartment Marilyn was occupying. When she pushed the buzzer outside of a door on the Eighth floor of an apartment building on Sutton Place South, a voice asked, "Who it it?"

"It's me," said my chaperon.

9

The lock clickety-clicked open, but when we went in, Marilyn was nowhere in sight. She had retreated into a bedroom. Her voice said to us through the door, "I'll be out in just seven minutes."

A publicity man to whom I had talked at Marilyn's studio in Hollywood had warned me, "She'll stand you up a couple of times before you meet her. Then she'll be late, and when I say late, I mean real late. You'll be so burned at her before she walks in that you'll wrap up your little voice-recording machine and get ready to leave at least three times — maybe four times — before she shows. But somebody will persuade you to wait, and finally Marilyn will come in, and before you know it, she'll have you wrapped up, too. For she's warmhearted, amusing, and likable, even if her lateness is a pain in the neck. And after that, if somebody says, 'That was mighty thoughtless of old Marilyn, keeping you waiting like that,' you'll want to slug him for being mean.

"But what you won't know," that studio publicity man went on, "is that while you're having hell's own headache waiting for her, whatever publicity worker is trying to get her to see you is having an even bigger headache. Marilyn will be telling that publicity worker that her stomach is so upset that she's been throwing up for hours; she hasn't been able to get her make-up on right; or she's got a bum deal in the wardrobe department and hasn't anything to wear."

So, in an effort to be jaunty and witty, when Marilyn said, through the closed door, "I'll be out in just seven minutes," I said, "I'll settle for eight."

Time was to prove it the unfunniest remark I've ever made.

One hour later I asked Lois Weber, "What do you suppose she's doing in there?"

"I've never had even one fairy godmother." PHIL BURCHMAN

PIN-UP GIRL — PEANUT SIZE. "I have had eleven or twelve sets of foster parents.... Some families kept me longer; others got tired of me in a short time. I must have made them nervous or something."

PHIL BURCHMAN

"One of the magazines I was on wasn't a man's magazine at all. It was called *Family Circle*. You buy it in supermarkets. I was holding a lamb with a pinafore. I was the one with the pinafore."

CULVER

"You know how it is," my publicity-girl chaperon said soothingly, "a girl has to put on her face."

"What has she got, two heads?" I asked politely.

A half hour later I suggested that Lois Weber go into the next room and see what was causing the delay.

Waiting for Lois Weber, I roamed the apartment. On a table lay a play manuscript. Typed on its cover was *Fallen Angels,* by Noel Coward. Among the books on the tables, which seemed in current use, were *Terry and Bernard Shaw;* Bernard Shaw and Mrs. Patrick Campbell: *Their Correspondence; Gertrude Lawrence as Mrs. A.,* by Richard Aldrich; Carl Sandburg's condensed *Abraham Lincoln.*

Mute evidence of Marilyn's widely publicized drama studies at the Actors' Studio, where she was said to be seeking out the secrets of artistic acting, was a copy of James Joyce's *Ulysses.* Several lines of dialogue from that volume had been penciled on a piece of paper, obviously to be recited by or to a group of drama students. Then the piece of paper had been thrust part way into the book. Lying on the floor was a large recording of John Barrymore as Hamlet.

That dialogue from *Ulysses* and the Barrymore recording represented one of the reasons why I was there. I'd read that Marilyn had gone "long-hair" and "art theaterish." I wanted to see for myself if she had. Just seeing it in print didn't make it true. Millions of words had been written about the blonde in whose living room I sat, but most of those words had been of the "authorized" or "with-her-blessing" variety. Several millions of them had appeared in fan magazines — after having first been O.K.'d by her studio's publicity department.

I'd read a lot of those words, but I still didn't understand this dame. I was sure that a lot of other people felt the same way about her and that for years, like myself, they'd been

13

asking themselves this question: "What's she *really* like?"

On top of that, they were probably asking themselves other questions — as I was doing.

"Why did she blow her marriage with Joe DiMaggio? Why did she walk out on a movie career that was paying her heavy money? Why did she duck California in favor of New York? Why, after she holed up there, did she attend the Actors' Studio — surely an unlikely place for a girl who, up to that time, was supposed to have done most of her acting with her hips?"

I hoped that when I talked to her she would tell me the answers to some of these things. Maybe I'd even see the "new Marilyn Monroe" I'd read about.

Lois Weber came back and reported: "She thinks the maid must have gone off with the top of her tapered slacks. She's running around without a top on."

I said, "I hope she doesn't trip. I don't want her to sprain her ankle or anything until after I've talked to her."

In an effort to keep me from brooding Lois Weber said, "The azalea people down in Wilmington, North Carolina, want her for a personal appearance in April, but I told them, 'Call me in April.' Who knows where she'll be then?"

The minutes crawled by and I thought of various things people had told me about Marilyn before I began that marathon wait in her New York apartment.

For instance, I'd asked one friend, high enough up in the Fox hierarchy, "Why do you think your studio brass let her come back to work for them after she walked out and stayed in New York for fifteen months?"

"Our attitude was that she'd never work on our lot again," he announced firmly; then he grinned at me and added, "Unless we needed her."

One of my longer talks was with Billy Wilder, the Holly-

14

wood director who directed Marilyn in *The Seven Year Itch*. Wilder is pungent, pithy, and not afraid to say what he thinks. I'd said to him that I'd read that when Marilyn had announced that she wanted to appear in a movie version of *The Brothers Karamazov*, some people hooted.

"The hooters were wrong," Wilder told me. "She meant that she wanted to play the part of Grushenka in that book, and people who haven't read the book don't know that Grushenka is a sex pot. People think this is a long-hair, very thick, very literary book, but Dostoevski knew what he was doing. There is nothing long-hair about Grushenka. Marilyn knows what she's doing, too. She would be a good Grushenka.

"It was after she said that she wanted to be in *The Brothers Karamazov*," Wilder went on, "that she started going to the Actors' Studio School in New York. She didn't do it for publicity. She is sincerely trying to improve herself, and I think that she should be admired for that. She could have sat here in Hollywood on her pretty little can and collected all of the money any ordinary actress would ever want, but she keeps trying."

Before dropping in to see Marilyn I also talked to a Hollywood publicity worker who had handled her relations with the public and the press for years. He talked to me quite frankly about Marilyn, and pulled no punches; but since it is unfair to quote such a source by name, I will call him Jones, and since "flack" is Hollywood slang for publicity man, I'll call him Flack Jones.

Jones worked for 20th Century-Fox during the years before Marilyn staged her walkout. Since then he has moved on to bigger — if not better — things. He has opened his own public-relations office, with branches in Paris and Rome. He is bald as a peeled egg. He is as broad as a small barn

15

door; a junior-size Mister Five-by-Five, and his eyes are framed by black-rimmed glasses instead of the tortoise-shell or clear plastic variety.

With Flack Jones I had discussed the question of whether Marilyn is mature. He made it clear that he "didn't mean physically mature."

"I remember the first day she came to work," he said. "She was in an Angora sweater way out to there. While we were shooting her in photography, the word got around and the boys rushed across the hall to get an eyeful. Next we did some layouts with her for picture magazines. We put her in a negligee, and she liked it so much she wouldn't take it off. She walked all over the lot in it, yelling, 'Yoo hoo' at strangers as far away as the third floor of the administration building. Pretty soon the whole third floor was looking down at her. The first and second floors were looking too."

Flack Jones did an abrupt shift into the present tense, "It's a bright, sunny day," he said; "the wind is blowing. She has Nature working with her. It has taken Nature quite a while to bring her to the ripe perfection she reaches on that day, but it finally makes it. The wind does the rest. She walks all over the lot, has a ball for herself, and so does everybody else."

With Flack Jones I discussed the famous Marilyn Monroe nude calendar, the one that had thrown the public into a tizzy when news of its existence was revealed.

"Curious thing about that calendar," Flack Jones said. "When it first came out, it had no bigger sale than any other nude calendar. You may not know it, but there's a steady sale for such calendars. You might think that there are too few places where you can hang them to make them worth while. But there're lots of places where they fit in very nicely

16

— trucker's havens, barbershops, bowling alleys, poolrooms, washrooms, garages, tool shops, taprooms, taverns — joints like that. The calendar people always publish a certain number of nude calendars along with standards like changing autumn leaves, Cape Cod fishermen bringing home their catch from a wintry sea, Old Baldy covered with snow. You're not in the calendar business unless you have a selection of sexy calendars. The sale of the one for which Marilyn posed was satisfactory, but not outstanding. It only became a 'hot number' when the public became familiar with it."

"A thing that fascinates me is this," I told Flack Jones: "The first time I ever saw her I was sitting with a friend in the Fox commissary and this girl came in with no make-up on. She was just wearing a blouse and skirt, and she sat against the wall. She bore no resemblance to anybody I'd ever seen before, but, to my amazement, my friend said, 'That's Marilyn Monroe.' So what I want to know is: Does she have to get into her Marilyn Monroe suit or put on her Marilyn Monroe face before she looks like Marilyn Monroe?"

"This is true of all platinum blondes or whatever you call the highly dyed jobs we have out here," Flack Jones said. "If their hair is not touched up and coiffured exactly right; if they're not gowned perfectly and their make-up is not one hundred per cent, they look gruesome. This is not peculiar to Monroe; it's peculiar to every other synthetic blonde I've ever known in picture business. There are very few blondes in Hollywood and, so far as I know, there have been no natural platinum blondes in mankind's history, except albinos. They are strictly a product of the twentieth century. They're created blondes, and when you create a

17

blonde you have to complete your creation with make-up and dramatic clothes, otherwise you've got only part of an assembly job."

I also talked to Milton Greene, the New York photographer who is vice-president of the new firm, Marilyn Monroe Productions, formed after Marilyn's last and longest walkout on Hollywood. Green asked me to put the initial "H" in his name, making it Milton H. Greene. "Would you mind very much?" he asked. "There're other Milton Greenes around New York who are also in the photography business." Looking at him, I couldn't help thinking of Nunnally Johnson's description: "Milton Greene," Nunnally had said, "is the only vice-president who hasn't wanted the president assassinated."

He told me he met Marilyn when he had gone to California to do a series of photographs of Grace Kelly, Elizabeth Taylor, Jean Simmons, and Marilyn Monroe. It hadn't been his idea to do anything *too* sexy. "After all," he said, "in a national magazine you can only expose so much of a girl, even if the girl is willing." Then he said thoughtfully, "Marilyn turned out to be different from the way I thought she'd be. More sensitive."

Greene had then gone to California on a second assignment. It was then that he had begun to think of doing a book of photographs of Marilyn.

"The book isn't out yet," Greene said, "but I'll show you a few of the pictures I've made for it. It will be Marilyn in different moods and settings, as if playing different parts."

He went to a shelf in his office and brought back a box of aluminum squares. Each square contained a color transparency. "Here's one where she looks as if she's in England," he said. "As you can see, she's wearing an Edwardian hat.

18

Here's one where she looks like Bernadette in *The Song of Bernadette*.

I looked at that one for a long time. It was a novel idea.

I also talked to a member of the Fox Studio Legal staff who told me a Monroe story I found provocative. "One day," he said, "she was in this office, and I said to her, 'It would be better for you to sign this contract this year instead of next. It will save you money.' She looked at me and said, 'I'm not interested in money. I just want to be wonderful.' Then she walked out."

The legal light looked at me helplessly and shrugged. "What do you suppose she meant by that?" he asked. I said I had no idea, but I'd try to find out.

Sitting now, waiting for Marilyn, in her Sutton Place apartment, I thought of the various interviews I had accumulated about her. And, remembering how honest, informative, and revealing many of them had been, I thought, *It's too bad all of the people I've talked to about Marilyn couldn't sit around one big table in the patio of the Beverly Hills Hotel and discuss her with me in a single bull session. If I could only snap my fingers and find myself in the middle of such a setup, it would make a much better story.*

In "all of the people" I included Marilyn, and myself, too.

So, placing my thumb and forefinger together, I snapped them.

There was a whirling before my eyes. The effect was that of shimmering white, as of someone rapidly twirling wedges of colored cardboard on a pinwheel. When the shimmering stopped, I was sitting at one of the large tables in the Polo Patio, an outdoor area that adjoins the Loggia and Polo Lounge at the Beverly Hills Hotel. Huge ceiling-to-floor glass doors are moved back and forth to let the outdoors

19

into the Loggia and the Loggia into the outdoors.

The floor of the Polo Patio is red brick. A green and white-striped canopy protects the banquettes on a setup level, and the canopy is held aloft by ivy-covered pergola posts. The patio focuses upon a Brazilian pepper tree, and the pepper tree, in turn, is surrounded by a low wall of whitewashed brick. The tables and chairs are white wrought iron. Cyclamens, fuchsias, and camellias in various shades of pink blend with the pink napery.

A blue jay that loves butter and cheese is a constant visitor. Among other fauna that finds the Polo Patio congenial is an ancient, oversized, weary yellow cat. His name is Rhubarb. Rhubarb is too war-worn to be interested in the jay. He is interested only in sleeping.

On my right in the scene I had snapped into existence; sat Billy Wilder. On my left was Marilyn. Next to her was Flack Jones. Across the table was Milton H. Greene.

The headwaiter, Rex, who is also Gene Autry's cousin, handed us menus. Flack Jones ordered cream chicken pancakes Suzette, a confection sprinkled with toasted almond slices; then baked.

I studied the menu and said, I'll have the cracked crab and the butterfly steak. And I'll have mustard sauce with the crab."

Then I said, "I think I'll have a bourbon milk punch while I'm waiting." Marilyn nibbled at a basketful of wholewheat wafers. Billy Wilder had a martini.

Milton H. Greene had coffee.

When the menus were whisked away, I turned to Marilyn and said, "I've heard your childhood referred to as 'the perfect Cinderella story.' "

"I don't know where they got that," she told me. "I haven't ended with a prince. I've never had even one fairy

20

Marilyn worked in a plane factory. The army photographers were around snapping. "Come outside," they told her. "We're going to take your picture. Don't you have a sweater?"

"Yes," she told them, "it so happens that I brought one with me."   PHIL BURCHMAN

"The basic idea was that this is a beautiful girl with a great body, although we had different approaches to it. Mountain shots, faked water-skiing shots — every type of approach we could think of. Picnicking, walking — anything a person does, we let her do it."

PHIL BURCHMAN

"Most of what I did while I was at Fox that first time was pose for stills. Publicity made up a story about how I was a baby-sitter who'd been baby-sitting for the casting director.... You'd think they would have had me at least a daddy-sitter."

PHIL BURCHMAN

godmother. Maybe they're thinking of a rags-to-riches routine. Not that I'm rich yet, but things are beginning to work out.

"My birth certificate reads Norma Jean Mortenson," she went on. "I was told that my father was killed in an automobile accident before I was born, so that is what I've always told people. There was no way I could check on that. I was brought up as an orphan."

I'd heard that she spent her childhood being farmed out to foster parents and to orphanages. Talking to her, I discovered that there'd been only one orphanage, although it was true about the foster parents. "I have had eleven or twelve sets of them," she told me. "I don't want to count them all again, to see whether there were really eleven or twelve. I hope you won't ask me to. It depresses me. Some families kept me longer; others got tired of me in a short time. I must have made them nervous or something."

She thought of something else. "I had one pair of foster parents and, when I was about ten they made me promise never to drink when I grew up, and I signed a pledge never to smoke or swear. My next foster family gave me empty whisky bottles for playthings. With them, and with empty cigarette packages, I played store. I guess I must have had the finest collection of empty whisky bottles and empty cigarette packages any girl ever had. I'd line them up on a plank beside the road, and when people drove along I'd say, 'Wouldn't you like some whisky?'

"I remember some of the people in the cars driving past my 'whisky' store saying, 'Imagine! Why, it's *terrible*.'

"Looking back, I guess I used to play-act all the time. For one thing, it meant I could live in a more interesting world than the one around me.

"The first family I lived with told me I couldn't go to

23

the movies because it was sinful," Marilyn said. "I listened to them say the world was coming to an end, and if I was doing something sinful when it happened, I'd go down below, below, below. So the few times I was able to sneak into a movie, I spent most of the time there praying the world wouldn't end while I was inside."

Apparently I had been misinformed about her first marriage, to a young man named Jim Dougherty. Somehow I'd gotten the idea that she'd married him while they were both in Van Nuys High School; that she'd got a "crush" on him because he was president of the student body there, a big wheel around the school.

"That's not true," she told me. "In the first place, he was twenty-one or twenty-two — well, at least he was twenty-one and already out of high school. So all I can say is that he must have been pretty dumb if he was still in high school when I married him. And I didn't have a crush on him, although he claimed that I did in a story he wrote about us. Along about that time I ran out of foster parents so I got married.

"That marriage ended in a divorce, but not until World War II was over. Jim is now a policeman. He lives in Reseda, in the San Fernando Valley, and he is happily married and has three daughters. But while he was away in the merchant marine, I worked in the dope room of a plane factory. I tried to make the best of it. The result was that I faced the worst of it.

"I guess you might say that I've led a haphazard life, but it really hasn't been so bad. Most of the people who are born in India or China or someplace lead lives that are much, much worse. The thing is I've taken it too hard. The truth is my life was tough, too, but if that's the kind of life you have, what can you do about it?

24

"That company not only made planes, it made parachutes. For a while I inspected parachutes. Then they quit letting us girls do that. They had the parachutes inspected on the outside, but I don't think it was because of my inspecting. Then I was in the dope room spraying dope on fuselages. Dope is liquid stuff, like banana oil and glue mixed.

"I was out on sick leave for a few days, and when I came back the Army photographers from the Hal Roach Studios, where they had the Army photographic headquarters, were around taking photographs and snapping and shooting while I was doping those ships. The Army guys saw me and asked, 'Where have *you* been?'

"'I've been on sick leave,' I said.

"'Come outside,' they told me. 'We're going to take your picture.'

"'I can't,' I said. 'The other ladies here in the dope room will give me trouble if I stop doing what I'm doing and go out with you.' That didn't discourage those Army photographers. They got special permission for me to go outside from Mr. Whosis, the president of the plant. For a while they posed me rolling ships; then they asked me, 'Don't you have a sweater?'

"'Yes,' I told them, 'it so happens that I brought one with me. It's in my locker.' After that I rolled ships around in a sweater. A photographer kept telling me, 'You should be a model,' but I thought he was flirting. Several weeks later, he brought the color shots he'd taken of me, and he said the Eastman Kodak Company has asked him, 'Who's your model, for goodness' sake?'

"So I began to think that maybe he wasn't kidding about how I ought to be a model. Then I found that a girl could make five dollars an hour modeling, which was different

25

from working ten hours a day for the kind of money I'd been making at the plane plant. And it was a long way from the orphanage, where I'd been paid five cents a week for working in the dining room or ten cents a month for working in the pantry. And out of those big sums a penny every Sunday had to go into the church collection. I never could figure why they took a penny from an orphan for that."

"What do you want to ask me about Marilyn Monroe?" Wilder asked me now. Looking at him, I found myself thinking that he looked like a smaller and thinner edition of Billiken, God of Things as They Ought to Be. Billiken was a household god of the early 1900's. He was once found on the mantels and the whatnots of many homes.

"One of the interesting things about this Monroe girl, to me," I said, "is that she seemed in danger of spoiling what had begun as a successful career by running away from it. I'd begun to ask myself: *How long can a movie actress afford to stay away from movie-making and still remain a star?* The mere strangeness of her staying away gets her a terrific press for a while and makes everyone in the country conscious of her, but is it possible to stay away so long that you're forgotten? Is that about to happen to Marilyn?"

"I don't know," Wilder said. "I can't tell you. There have been examples in the past of movie stars shaking the diamond dust of Hollywood from their feet for one reason or another, but I'd rather not make any comparisons. If you take the case of Garbo, I think that she has gained in stature by staying away; however, I'm not comparing the quality or depth of one actress with another."

"Could Garbo come back now if she wanted to?" I asked.

"I think so, although I don't know," Wilder said. "But I don't think there is any danger of Marilyn sinking into

26

"The formation of my lids must make them look heavy or else I'm thinking of something. Sometimes I'm thinking of men; other times I'm thinking of some man in particular. It's easier to look sexy when you're thinking of some man in particular." PHIL BURCHMAN

Marilyn's best friend and encourager was an agent, Johnny Hyde. He was little physically, but he was Marilyn's good friend. He could and did do things for her. Johnny wanted to marry her and Marilyn wouldn't do it. PHIL BURCHMAN

oblivion, because a thing like her doesn't come along every minute."

I asked, "What do you mean, 'a thing like her'?"

"She has what I call flesh impact," Wilder said. "It's very rare. Three I remember are Clara Bow, Jean Harlow, and Rita Hayworth. Such girls have flesh which photographs like flesh. You feel you can reach out and touch it."

During the first few moments of my talk with Wilder, it seemed odd to be discussing Marilyn right in front of her, just as if she weren't there; but watching her across the table gave me a different idea. From the intent look on her face none of us gathered there could possibly be anyone more interested in the discussion than she was.

This girl, I thought, *is anxious to hear anything about herself — both praise and criticism — if only she can use it for guidance and self-improvement.*

"I've heard that it's a moot question as to whether Marilyn's an actress or not," I said.

"I've heard that too," he replied. "It's also moot whether you have to be an actor or an actress to be a success in pictures. I'm sure you've heard the theory that there are two kinds of stars — those who can act and those who are personalities. I'll take a personality any time. I can mention many indifferently paid actors who can act rings around the stars who get $250,000 a picture, plus a percentage. The highly paid ones never went to an actors' lab or studio or workshop, but something comes down from the screen to you when you see them, in a way that it doesn't always come from the indifferently paid actors, although they may be perfect at their jobs."

"It's nothing against them or for them," Flack Jones put in. "It's the way this business is put together. If the public likes a personality, he or she goes over. You take Tab Rock,"

29

he said (only Tab Rock is not the name he used). "Old Tab's a terrific personality. I doubt if he's ever made a flop picture, but he's never made a really good picture.

"This fellow can't pick up his hat without instruction, yet he's always picking up villians and throwing them across a bar singlehanded. He can clean up any tough barroom on the frontier, but he can't clean up a kitchen. He's a nice guy, but no one has ever called him an actor. You take Lloyd Nolan now, or Van Heflin or Fredric March. That's acting for you. You believe them. There are lights and shades and meaning to what they do. But when old Tab Rock comes on the screen, he's got to throw somebody around to prove his art. He can do this quicker than anybody in Hollywood, and this is his great value."

"He sounds brave," I said.

"No one is braver or more scornful about it," Flack Jones said. "His bravery is without parallel in the industry. He's the only man I ever saw who could take a forty-five to the Orient or to the Near East and clean the whole mess up in a day or two. He never fails. That's the difference between being a personality and an actor."

My eye wandered for a moment. At a nearby table was Hernando Courtright, resident manager of the hotel. With him was Neal McCarthy, a movie-colony lawyer. At another table sat John Wayne with his business partner, Bob Fellows. Wayne was putting away a non-weight-reducing steak and sliced tomatoes. Greg Peck was lunching with John Ford.

"Aside from whether Marilyn's an actress or not," Wilder went on, "she's got this lovely little shape, it twitches excitingly, and the public likes to watch it, either coming toward them or going away from them. There are two schools of thought about her — those who like her and those

30

who attack her — but they both are willing to pay to watch her. Their curiosity is good for eighty cents or a dollar and a quarter or whatever the price of the ticket is."

He shook his head thoughtfully. "And she went back East to study at a slow-take arty place, where they feature understatement. Here's a girl who's built herself a career on overstating something, and she's made up her mind to understate. It won't be long before we'll know whether she's right or wrong, and whether she needs the wardrobe department and the hairdressing department as much as she needs artistic lines to say. It'll be interesting to watch, and I hope it works out the way she wants it to, but so far the lines the public really wants from her are not written in English. They are her curves."

I told myself that it would be useful to draw Marilyn into the conversation, so I said to her, "You look well in black."

She agreed with me. She added that she also looked well in white, beige, and red. "If I wear just straight beige," she said, "I don't get mixed up with anything."

That baffled me, but I told myself that it would have meant something to another girl.

I remembered that each male friend I had told I was doing a story about Marilyn had asked me, "Can I go along to hold your notebook?" or "You call *that* work?" or "You mean you get *paid* for that?"

Apparently they felt that if they failed to go into a blood-bubbling, he-man routine at a drop of her name, their maleness was suspect.

I told Marilyn of this phenomenon. "How do you explain it?" I asked her. "Have you become a symbol of sex?"

She gave my query some thought before answering. "There are people to whom other people react, and other people who do nothing for people," she said. "I react to

31

men, too, but I don't do it because I'm trying to prove that I'm a woman. Personally I react to Marlon Brando. He's a favorite of mine.

"There are two kinds of reactions. When you see some people you say, 'Gee!' When you see other people you say, 'Ugh!' If that part about my being a symbol of sex is true, it ought to help out at the box office, but I don't want to be commercial about it."

Then quite seriously she said, "After all, it's a responsibility, too — being a symbol, I mean."

I told her that I'd heard that among the titles bestowed upon here were The Woo-Woo Girl, Miss Cheesecake, The Girl with the Horizontal Walk.

She said that it was true that she had been labeled all of those things — and more. "But," she said, "I don't get what they mean by 'horizontal walk.' Naturally I know what walking means — anybody knows that — and horizontal means not vertical. So what?"

I thought about trying to blueprint it for her. Then I decided not to.

She went on, "When Jane Russell and I were together in the cast of Gentlemen Prefer Blondes, we were asked to put our footprints in wet concrete in front of Grauman's Chinese Theater, along with the dent left by Jimmy Durante's nose and the print of one of Betty Grable's legs. I suggested that Jane lean over the wet cement and that I sit down in it and we could leave our prints that way, but my idea was vetoed. After that I suggested that Grauman's use a diamond to dot the 'I' in the Marilyn I scratched in the wet concrete. They finally compromised on dotting it with a rhinestone, but some sight-seer chiseled that rhinestone out."

I queried Marilyn about a photograph taken of her clad

32

"There were different poses — outdoors, indoors, but mostly just sitting looking over the Pacific. That brought in the swimsuit idea. You didn't see much ocean, but you saw a lot of me." PHIL BURCHMAN

"She has what I call flesh impact. It's very rare. Three I remember are Clara Bow, Jean Harlow, and Rita Hayworth. Such girls have flesh which photographs like flesh. You feel you can reach out and touch it."

PHIL BURCHMAN

skimpily but neatly in a burlap potato bag. I'd been told that over four hundred newspapers had printed that picture, which must have established an all-time record for pictures of girls taken in potato sacks.

"Why was that picture taken?" I asked.

"Because I wore a certain red dress to a party at the Beverly Hills Hotel," she told me. "It was a beautiful dress. It cost a fortune. I got it at I. Magnin's. It was a copy of a French original. But one lady columnist wrote that I was cheap and vulgar in it and that I would have looked better in a potato sack. So, somebody in studio publicity asked, 'So O.K., why don't we shoot old Marilyn in a potato sack?'

"That was fine with me, as long as they let me wear long, dangling earrings and a bracelet four inches wide. I don't know about the more than four hundred newspapers, but I do know that shot was printed all over the country. As a result, a potato company in Twin Falls, Idaho, sent me a sack of potatoes. There was a potato shortage on then, and the boys in publicity stole them all. I never saw one. It just goes to show why I always ask, 'Can you trust a publicity man or can't you?' "

"They tell me that you devote hours to selecting and editing pin-up pictures of yourself," I told Marilyn.

"I haven't so far," she told me. "But maybe it's time I started. At least I'd like to have my pictures not look worse than I do. I'd like some resemblance to me, even if only a little bit. With some photographers, all they ask is that a picture doesn't look blurred like I'd moved while they were taking it. If it's not blurry they print it."

"Somewhere I read that at least half of the photographs taken of you are killed as being too revealing," I said.

She frowned a frown of frustration. "That's the Johnston Office for you," she sighed. "The Johnston Office kills prac-

35

tically everything taken of me, and what the Johnston Office passes the studio retouches. After one sitting they killed twenty-eight of thirty poses of me. The Johnston Office spends a lot of time worrying about whether a girl has cleavage or not. It seems to me that they ought to worry if she *doesn't* have any. That really would upset people.

"I don't know what their reasoning is," she went on, with a puzzled air. "Maybe they expect girls to look like boys."

"I've read that your measurements are thirty-seven, twenty-three, thirty-four," I told her, "but there must be more to your success than your statistics, which are no more eye-filling than those of many of your Hollywood contemporaries."

"If you're talking about my lower hips, they're thirty-seven inches," she said. "If you're talking about my upper hips, they're thirty-four."

Eying her, I tried to decide where her "upper hip" left off and "lower hip" began. I gave up.

"Nowadays," she said, "there seems to be a vogue for women with twenty-twenty-twenty figures. In the high-style magazines you see models with their hip bones sticking out if nothing else. But I'm a woman, and the longer I am one the more I enjoy it. And since I *have* to be a woman I'm glad I'm me. I've been asked, 'Do you mind living in a man's world?' I always answer, 'Not as long as I can be a woman in it.'"

"How did you happen to sign your first movie contract?" I asked.

She tossed a cascade of white-blond tresses from her right eye and explained, "I had appeared on five magazine covers. Mostly men's magazines."

I asked what she meant by men's magazines?

36

"Magazines," she said, "with cover girls who aren't flat-chested. I was on *See* four or five months in a row. Each time they changed my name. One month I was Norma Jean Dougherty—they used my first husband's name. The second month I was Jean Norman. I don't know what-all names they used, but I must have looked different each time.

"There were different poses—outdoors, indoors, but mostly just sitting looking over the Pacific. That brought in the swimsuit idea. You looked at those pictures and you didn't see much ocean, but you saw a lot of me.

"One of the magazines I was on wasn't a man's magazine at all. It was called *Family Circle.* You buy it in supermarkets. I was holding a lamb with a pinafore. I was the one with the pinafore. But on most covers I had on things like a striped towel. The towel was striped because the cover was to be in color and the stripes were the color, and there was a big fan blowing on the towel and on my hair. That was right after my first divorce, and I needed to earn a living bad. I couldn't type. I didn't know how to do *anything.* So Howard Hughes had an accident."

I wondered if I'd missed something. Apparently I hadn't.

"He was in the hospital," she went on, "and Hedda Hopper wrote in her column: 'Howard Hughes must be recuperating because he sent out for photographs of a new girl he's seen on five different magazines.' Right after that Howard Hughes's casting director got my telephone number, and he got in touch with me and he said Howard Hughes wanted to see me."

I went back in my mind over the long list of stars and starlets in whom Hughes had betrayed an interest, but I couldn't remember Marilyn's name on the list.

"But he must have forgotten or changed his mind or

37

something," she said, "because instead of going to see him, I went over to the Fox Studio with a fellow named Harry Lipton, who handled my photography modeling.

"Expensive cars used to drive up beside me when I was standing on a street corner or walking on a sidewalk, and the driver would say, 'I could do something for you in pictures. How would you like to be a Goldwyn girl?'

"I figured those guys in those cars were trying for a pickup," she said, "and I got an agent so I could say to those fellows, 'See my agent.' That's how I happened to be handled by Harry Lipton."

Harry took her to see Ivan Kahn, then head of Fox's talent department, and also to see Ben Lyon, who was doing a talent-scouting job for Fox.

"When Ben saw me," Marilyn told me," he said, 'You're the first girl I've discovered since Jean Harlow who I'm sure will make it.' "

I asked her how it happened that she changed her name from Norma Jean Dougherty to Marilyn Monroe.

"Ben Lyon renamed me," she said. "Ben said that I reminded him of two people, Jean Harlow and somebody else he remembered, a girl named Marilyn Miller. When all the talk began about renaming me, I asked if please could I keep my mother's maiden name — Monroe. So the choice was whether to call me Jean Monroe or Marilyn Monroe. Marilyn won. That very evening I was in a parade when some kids asked me for my autograph. I didn't know how to spell Marilyn, and I had to ask a stranger how to spell it."

"What happened when she came to your studio?" I asked Flack Jones.

"Actually she came twice," he said. "The first time was in 1946. We did our best with her then, but she just hadn't grown up enough. She was great as far as looks went, but

Nobody can write dialogue
for her which could pos-
sibly sound half as much
like her as the dialogue she
thinks up for herself.

PHIL BURCHMAN

Marilyn is an international symbol of sex—so complex she has complexes about complexes.　　　　　PHIL BURCHMAN

she didn't know how to make the most of her looks or what to do with them. That came to her with practice. Not that you have to grow up mentally to be a star," he added. "In fact, it can be a holdback. It might even defeat you. Stars who are grown up mentally are in the minority.

"But the thing was," he said, "we had no stories lying around at that time in which she would appear to good advantage."

"So what did you do?" I asked.

He speared a forkful of cream chicken pancakes Suzette, and replied, "We tried her out in a picture or two in which she played bit parts — secretaries; the pretty girl in the background. Stuff like that. Then we let her go, and she went over to RKO and did a picture with Groucho."

The effort of remembering wrinkled Jones's brow. "In that Marx Brothers picture she was cast as a bosomy mechanical bunny, romping about the sound stage a couple of jumps ahead of a posse of pursuing Marxes."

"I didn't see that film," I said, "but you'd think with all the Marx Brothers chasing her the fun would have been fast and furious."

"The trouble was that while the Marx Brothers always chased a dame in their pictures," Flack Jones told me, "they never caught up with the dame. Usually the dame never became a star either, so the whole thing was a waste of time. It was amusing while you were watching it, but unfortunately, the girls usually outran both the Marx boys and a career.

"When she finished that picture she went over to Columbia for a couple of shows; but she didn't click, and they released her too. After that she was around town for a while going broke. It was then that she posed for that calendar."

Marilyn gave me her own version of Flack Jones's story:

41

"I stayed on at Fox for a year before they let me go. During that time they put me in a picture called *Scudda Hoo, Scudda Hay*. Then they took me out of it, but they left me in the cast of characters — you know, that thing that appears on the screen at the beginning of each picture. At least they *almost* took me out of it. Part of my back showed in one scene, but nobody knew it except me and some particular friends of mine.

"Most of what I did while I was at Fox that first time was pose for stills. Publicity made up a story about how I was a baby-sitter who'd been baby-sitting for the casting director and that's how I was discovered. They told me to say that, although it strictly wasn't true. You'd think that they would have used a little more imagination and that they would have had me at least a daddy-sitter."

Flack Jones wriggled on his white iron chair and took up the chronological burden. "After that Groucho job, she went to Metro and appeared in *The Asphalt Jungle*, directed by John Huston," he said. "Marilyn's role was small. She was only a walk-on, but she must have looked good to Darryl Zanuck, for when he saw it, he re-signed her.

"*Asphalt Jungle* was one of those gangster things. There was a crooked legal mouthpiece in it, a suave fellow, played by Louis Calhern. Marilyn was his 'niece'; which was a nice word for 'keptie.' She'd say a few lines of dialogue; then she'd look up at him with those big eyes of hers and call him 'Uncle.'"

I said that I'd been trying to find a phrase that would describe her walk, but that I hadn't been able to.

"I can't help you there," Flack Jones said. "I've heard the words 'quivering' and 'trembling buttocks' used in connection with her walk, but I don't know a description which *really* does the job. But she walked across the screen a couple

42

or three times and that did it. Her walk attracted a lot of attention — a whole lot."

I decided to put it to the lady who owned the walk, so I said to Marilyn, "I've heard that in *Asphalt Jungle* you displayed a highly individual way of walking and that it called attention to you and made you stand out. I've heard a lot of people try to describe the way you walk. Some of these descriptions are pretty lurid. How do you describe it?"

She leaned forward, placed her elbows on the glass-topped table, and cupped her chin in her palms. She was very effective that way.

"I've never deliberately done anything about the way I walk," she said. "I just walk to get there. I wasn't even deliberate about it in the picture, *Niagara*, where people said that I walked wiggly and wobbly. I don't know what they mean. I just walk. I've never wiggled deliberately in my life, but all my life I've had trouble with people who say that I do wiggle deliberately. In high school the other girls would ask me, 'Why do you walk down the hall *that* way? I guess the boys must have been watching me and it made the other girls mad — but I said, 'I don't know what you mean. I learned to walk when I was ten months old and I've been walking this way ever since.'"

"In *Niagara*, Marilyn was only doing what the director wanted her to," Flack Jones said. "It wasn't her prerogative to cut a picture or to tell the director not to point the camera at her behind during a long walk away from the lens across cobblestones. I challenge any girl to walk down a cobblestone street in high heels without wiggling at least a little bit as she picks her heels up and lays them down."

Rex, the headwaiter, brought a telephone over to our table and plugged it into a nearby plug. "It is for you, Mr. Wilder," he said. Billy began to mumble into it. I tried not to eavesdrop, but I couldn't help overhear a mention of his latest film, the Lindbergh story, *The Spirit of St. Louis*.

"What does Marilyn do best?" I asked Flack Jones. "Is her walk her greatest asset?"

Jones regarded the feathery top of a slender palm tree swaying above the hotel roof as if searching for an answer there.

"She does two things beautifully," he said. "She walks and she stands still. In addition she has wit enough to buy her clothes one or two sizes too small for her. With a chassis like hers, this infuriates women and intrigues guys. From a woman's standpoint, there is no subtlety in such gowns. I remember when Marilyn came to a fancy affair one night in a number which fitted her like a silk-thin banana peel, and the other women there thought she was outrageous."

"How did Marilyn react to their reaction?" I asked.

"Comments were made about that gown in a gossip column," Jones told me, "and Marilyn asked me, 'What should I have done?'

"I said, 'Look, Marilyn, the men loved it. Any time you quit dressing for men you're out of business. Pay no attention to what that gossip-column cat said. You're a man's woman, so dress for men, not for other women. If you ever get that out of your curly noggin you're cooked.'

"Women always hate the obvious in sex," he said, "and men love it." Apparently Flack Jones had given this matter a lot of thought. He had even worked out a philosophy about it. "Guys are instinctively awkward and blundering and naïve — even the worldly-wise ones. Subtlety in sex baffles them. Not only that, but they don't have the time. Women who are not supporting a husband have all the time in the world for it. But men have other things to do, like making a dollar; and they like their love-making without

44

preliminaries which last four or five hours. Marilyn instinctively knows this. She is a very down-to-earth, a very straightforward girl."

I chose between a forkful of hashed brown potatoes and a wedge of butterfly steak. Then I asked Jones, "How does a big studio start a campaign to build up a personality like Marilyn?"

I thought it would be a change of pace if I got him off of the libido. I was wrong. It was too difficult to do. He told me, "We took her to the beach with a lot of wardrobe changes, but the basic idea was that this is a beautiful girl with a great body, and that idea was always the same, although we did have different approaches to it. We had color shots, he had black-and-white shots, we had mountain shots, we had field shots, faked water-skiing shots — every type of approach we could think of. Picknicking, walking — anything a person does, we let her do it. When we began to see what she did best, then we concentrated on it."

"When did you first notice her impact on the public?" I asked him.

"Once we got her rolling, it was like a tidal wave," he said. We began to release some photographs of her, and as soon as they appeared in print, we had requests for more from all over the world. We had the newspapers begging for art; then the photo syndicates wanted her; then the magazines began to drool. For a while we were servicing three or four photos to key newspapers all over the world once a week — and that was before she had appeared in a picture.

"Once this building-up process started," Flack Jones explained, "other people became interested in her. We called up the top cameramen around town who had their own outlets, and we told them what we had, and we asked them if they'd like to photograph her. They said. 'Ho, boy, yes.'

45

"We told them what the deal was," Flack Jones went on. "We said, 'We think this girl has got a great future; she's beautiful, her chassis is great, and are you interested?' Each guy had his own idea of what he wanted, and he let his imagination play upon her. This is the way such things get done. They're not created by one person. They're the creation of all of the press representatives who cover Hollywood for all the publications in the world, which means about 350 people.

"Everybody in the studio publicity department worked on her." Jones ticked them off on his fingertips. "The picture division, the magazine division, the fan-magazine division, the planters who plant the columnists, the radio planters, and so forth. Then, when you make a motion picture, a 'unit man' or 'unit woman' is assigned to cover its shooting, and he or she handles publicity for that film alone. In addition, the whole department works on the same picture. Our department is highly specialized, but each specialist in each department makes his contribution to the personality we're erecting in the public's mind."

"Ive met a couple of press agents who've been unit men on Marilyn's films," I said.

"But the unit man is not always the same for a certain star's pictures," Jones said. "Sonia Wilson's been unit woman on Monroe pictures, and Frankie Neal's been a unit man on her pictures, but Roy Craft has been her unit man more than anyone else. Roy likes her. He gets along with her fine."

There was something else I wanted to know. "In addition to distributing her photographs," I asked, "did you have her show up at different places where you thought her appearance would do her good?"

"We took her to all of the cocktail parties we thought

46

It has been said that she dislikes being interviewed by women reporters, but that it's different with gentlemen of the press because "we have a mutual appreciation of being male and female." (About eating with a man) "I don't give the food much thought." (About resting) "I sit down the way I feel."

PHIL BURCHMAN

"As for my mouth being open all the time, I even sleep with it open. I know, because it's open when I wake up. I never consciously think of my mouth, but I do consciously think about what I'm thinking about."

PHIL BURCHMAN

were important," Flack Jones said. "For instance, one picture magazine had its annual cocktail party, and we told Marilyn she ought to show so we could introduce her to various editors, columnists, and radio and television people. She waited until everybody else had arrived; then she came in in this red gown I've told you about. That gown became famous. It got more mileage than any other gown in the history of picture business, although it finished second in space-grabbing to the dress Marlene Dietrich wore at Las Vegas a year or two ago."

Flack Jones took a long drag of his iced coffee — it had been served to him in a triple-size Old-Fashioned glass — and said, "When she came in, everybody stopped doing what they were doing and their eyes went, 'Boing, boing!' The publisher of the magazine who was picking up the tab for the party shook hands with her a long, long time, while Marilyn talked to him as if he was the only one in the room. After a while he turned to one of his associate editors and said, 'We ought to have a picture of this little girl in our book.' Then he looked at her again and said, 'Possibly we should have her on the cover.'"

Flack Jones grinned. "So that's the way things went," he said. "Some months there were as many as fifteen or sixteen covers of her on the newsstands at once. She came back to the Fox lot in 1950 to appear in *All About Eve,* but she was still not anyone's great big brilliant discovery until we got our still cameras focused on her and started spreading those Marilyn Monroe shots all over the universe."

"What did she do in *All About Eve?*" I asked. "I don't remember."

"She was the dumb broad who walked into a party at Bette Davis's place leaning on George Sanders' arm," he said. "There was dialogue which showed you that Sanders

49

was a dramatic critic. He brought this beautiful dish Marilyn in, and he sighted a producer played by Gregory Ratoff. Sanders pointed at Ratoff and said to Marilyn, 'There's a real live producer, honey. Go do yourself some good.' So Marilyn went off to do herself some good while Sanders stayed in his own price class with Bette."

Jones clinked the ice in his coffee thoughtfully against the sides of his glass and said, "There was one wonderful scene in which Marilyn was sitting at the foot of the stairs with this producer. He was telling her that he's going to do another picture when all at once all hell broke loose. Bette Davis threw a tantrum, then came down the stairs and denounced Anne Baxter in screaming hysterics. But old Marilyn just sat there wide-eyed; still the completely unaware blonde, paying no attention to the terrifying excitement, bitterness, and hatred going on all around her."

He considered what he'd said for a moment, then added, "She was good at it. I still didn't know whether she was acting or not."

"There's a thing I'd like to know," I said. "When did this business of her making all of those wonderful Monroe cracks start?"

"You mean when somebody asked her what she wears in bed and she said, 'Chanel Number Five'?" Flack Jones asked.

"Yes," I replied. "And I've read that she said she dislikes being interviewed by women reporters, but that it's different with gentlemen of the press because, as she put it, "we have a mutual appreciation of being male and female.' And that she said about eating with a man: 'I don't give the food much thought.' And on resting: ' I sit down the way I feel.' "

Flack Jones said, "You will find some who will tell you that her humor content seemed to pick up the moment she

50

signed a contract with the studio, and that anybody in the department who had a smart crack lying around handy gave it to her. Actually, there were those who thought that more than the department was behind it. 'Once you launch such a campaign,' they said, 'it stays launched. It's like anyone who has a smart crack to pass along attributing it to a George Jessel or to a Dorothy Parker or whoever is currently smart and funny.'

"There was even a theory that the public contributed some of Marilyn's cracks by writing to columnists like Sidney Skolsky, or Herb Stein on Army Archerd, Mike Connolly, and give them gags and they'd attribute them to Marilyn Monroe, and so on around town. But the majority of the thinking was that our publicity department gave her her best cracks."

"Like what?" I asked.

"Like for instance," he said. "I'll have to lead up to it; as you know, in this business you can be destroyed by one really bad story, one honest-to-John stinker — although that's not as true as it used to be — and when the story broke that Marilyn had posed in the nude for a calendar, the studio decided that the best thing to do was to announce the facts immediately instead of trying to pretend they didn't exist. They said that Marilyn was broke at the time and that she'd posed to pay her room rent, which was true. Then, to give it the light touch, when she was asked, 'Didn't you have *anything* on at all when you were posing for that picture?' we were supposed to have told her to say, 'I had the radio on.' "

Flack Jones paused for a moment. "I'm sorry to disagree," he said firmly, "but she makes up those cracks herself. Certainly that 'Chanel Number Five' was her own."

Marilyn smiled gratefully. "He's right. It *was* my own,"

51

she said. "The other one — the calendar crack — I made when I was up in Canada. A woman came up to me and asked, 'You mean to say you didn't have anything on when you had that calendar picture taken?' I drew myself up and told her, 'I did, too, have something on. I had the radio on.'"

Flack Jones insisted, "Give her a minute to think and Marilyn is the greatest little old ad-lib artist you ever saw. She blows it in sweet and it comes out that way. One news magazine carried a whole column of her quotes I'd collected, and every one of them was her own. There've been times when I could have made plenty of face in this industry by claiming that I put some of those cracks into her mouth, but I didn't do it. This girl makes her own quotables.

"She'll duck a guy who wants to interview her as long as she can, but when she finally gets around to it, she concentrates on trying to give him what he wants — something intriguing and amusing, and off-beat. She's very bright at it.

"For example, a writer was commissioned to write a story for her for a magazine," Jones said. "The subject was to be what Marilyn eats and how she dresses. As I recall it, the title was to be 'How I Keep My Figure,' or maybe it was 'How I Keep in Shape.' The writer talked to Marilyn; then ghosted the article. He wrote it very much the way she'd told it to him, but he had to pad it a little because he hadn't had too much time with her. As a result, in one section of his article he had her saying that she didn't like to get out in the sun and pick up a heavy tan because a heavy tan loused up her wardrobe by confusing the colors of her dresses and switching around what they did for her.

"The article read good to me, so I took it over to Marilyn for her corrections and approval. Most of the stuff was the routine thing about diet, but when she came to the part

52

"In the high-style magazines you see models with their hip bones sticking out if nothing else. But I'm a woman, and the longer I am one the more I enjoy it. And since I *have* to be a woman I'm glad I'm me."   PHIL BURCHMAN

It was another actress who accused Marilyn of wearing falsies. Her answer to that is: "Those who know me better know better. That's all."

PHIL BURCHMAN

about 'I don't like suntan because it confuses the coloring of my wardrobe,' she scratched it out.

" 'What's the matter?' " I asked.

" 'That's ridiculous,' she said. 'Having a suntan doesn't have anything to do with my wardrobe.'

"I said, "You've got to say *something*, Marilyn. After all, the guy's article is pretty short as it is.'

"She thought for a minute; then she wrote, 'I do not suntan because I like to feel blonde all over.' I saw her write that with her own little pencil.

"The magazine which printed that story thought her addition so great they picked it out and made it into a subtitle. She'd managed to transpose an ordinary paragraph about wardrobe colors into a highly exciting, and beautiful, sexy mental image. And some guys have said to me, 'Why that dumb little broad couldn't have thought that up. You thought it up, Jones. You know you did!' I wish I could say, 'Yeah, I did,' but I didn't."

He said musingly, "Feeling blond all over is a state of mind. I should think it would be a wonderful state of mind if you're a girl.

"One reason why she's such a good interview," Flack Jones went on, poking his shrimp salad, "is that she uses her head during such sessions. She tries to say something that's amusing and quotable, and she usually does. When I worked with Marilyn I made it a practice to introduce her to a writer and go away and leave her alone, on the grounds that a couple of grown people don't need a press agent tugging at their sleeves while they're getting acquainted. If her interviews have been any good, it's her doing.

"One day she gave a tape interview and it was all strictly ad-lib," he said. "I know, because I had a hard time getting it set up. I think it was for a man who was doing one of

55

those fifteen-minute radio interviews in Hollywood, to be broadcast afterward across the country. We had a frantic time trying to set up the time with her, but finally he got his recorder plugged in, and the first question he asked her he pitched her a curve. He wanted to know what she thought of the Stanislavsky school of dramatic art. Believe it or not, old Marilyn unloaded on him with a twelve-minute dissertation on Stanislavsky which rocked him back on his heels."

"Does she believe in the Stanislavsky method?" I asked.

"She agreed with Stanislavsky on certain points," Jones said. "She disagreed on others, and she explained why. It was one of the most enlightening discussions on the subject I've ever heard. It came in over the radio a couple of nights later, and everybody who listened said, 'Oh, yeah? Some press agent wrote that interview for her.' My answer to that was, 'What press agent knows that much about Stanislavsky?' I know I don't."

"There are a few million readers who've never heard of Stanislavsky either," I said. "What are his doctrines?"

"I've told you I don't know," Flack Jones said, "but after hearing Marilyn discuss it, I think it goes something like this: The Stanislavsky school is a thing where you feel the role. They tell you to make like a rock or like a bird, and you sit there and think you're a rock on a hillside or you pretend you're a bird winging through the sky. You're a swallow and God's eye is on you. It's not necessarily done with gestures, but with inner feeling. At least, that's the way I understand it. I have a shallow mind and I've never figured it out fully, but as a technique of dramatic art it's widely practiced."

Billy Wilder finished his martini and I thought I heard

56

him tell our waiter that he was ready for his Frank Folsom hamburger.

He agreed with Jones. "I think that she thinks up those funny things herself," he said. Wilder's Austrian background gives his phrases an off-beat rhythm, but his way of talking picks up extra meaning and eloquence because of its differentness.

"I think also that she says those funny things without realizing that they're so funny," Wilder said. "One very funny thing she said involves the fact that she has great difficulties in remembering her lines. Tremendous difficulties. I've heard of one director who wrote her lines on a blackboard, then kept that blackboard just out of camera range where she could see it. The odd thing is that if she has a long scene for which she has to remember a lot of words, she's fine once she gets past the second word. If she gets over that one little hump, there's no trouble. Then, too, if you start a scene and say, 'Action!' and hers is the first line, it takes her ten or fifteen seconds to gather herself. Nothing happens during those fifteen seconds. To a director it seems a very long time."

"How about an example of when she bogged down on a second word," I asked.

"For instance, if she had to say, 'Good morning, Mr. Sherman,' " Wilder told me, "she couldn't get out the word 'morning.' She would say, 'Good . . .' and stick. But once she got 'morning' out, she'd be good for two pages of dialogue. It's just that sometimes she trips over mental stumbling blocks at the beginning of a scene.

"Another director should be telling you this next story, not me," Wilder said. "The one it happened to. This other director was directing her in a scene and she couldn't get the lines out. It was just muff, muff, muff, and take, take, take. Finally, after Take Thirty-two, he took her to one side, patted her on the head, and said, 'Don't worry, Marilyn honey. It'll be all right.' She looked up into his face with those big, wide eyes of hers and asked, 'Worry about what? She had no idea that thirty-two takes is a lot of takes.''

I turned to Marilyn and said, "I've tried hard to trace those famed remarks attributed to you and find out who originated them. Are they really yours or did somebody else put them into your mouth? Billy Wilder and Flack Jones, who know you, swear that you ad-lib them.''

"Those remarks are mine," Marilyn told me. "Nobody in publicity thought of them. If they were going to try, they'd think of something corny. Sometimes I looked at what they reported me as saying and I said, 'No! No! No!'

"Take that Chanel Number Five remark," she went on. "Somebody was always asking me, 'What do you sleep in Marilyn? Do you sleep in P.J.'s? Do you sleep in a nightie? Do you sleep raw, Marilyn?' It's one of those questions which make you wonder how to answer it. Then I remembered that the truth is the easiest way out, so I said, 'I sleep in Chanel Number Five,' because I do.''

She went on, "Or you take the columnist, Earl Wilson, when he asked me if I have a bedroom voice, and I said, 'I don't talk in the bedroom, Earl.' Then, thinking back over that remark, I thought maybe I ought to say something else to clarify it, so I added, '. . . because I live alone.' ''

I told her that I had met one or two people who thought her naïve and unsophisticated. "If you ask me, I think I'm a mixture," she told me. "Of what I don't know. One thing, I'm continually off balance. Sometimes I feel very simple and sometimes not.''

Flack Jones raised his voice above the cackle from the

58

"She has Nature working with her. It takes Nature quite a while to bring her to the ripe perfection she reaches, but it finally makes it."

PHIL BURCHMAN

"I wore a certain red dress to a party at the Beverly Hills Hotel ... But one columnist wrote that I was cheap and vulgar in it and that I would have looked better in a potato sack. So, somebody in studio publicity asked, 'So O.K., why don't we shoot old Marilyn in a potato sack?'"

TWENTIETH CENTURY-FOX

other tables, and said, "I'm no psychiatrist or psychologist, or whatever they call those head-feelers, but I think that Marilyn has a tremendous inferiority complex. I think that she's scared to death all the time. I know that she needs and requires attention and that she needs and requires somebody to tell her that she's doing well, and that she's extremely grateful for a pat on the back."

"Name me a patter," I said.

"For example," he said, "when we put her under contract for the second time, her best friend and encourager was an agent, Johnny Hyde. Johnny was then with the William Morris Agency, although he subsequently died of a heart attack. He was a little guy physically, but he was Marilyn's good friend, and, in spite of his lack of size, I think that she had a father fixation on him.

"I don't want to get involved in the psycholoy of all this," Flack Jones continued, "because it was a very complicated problem, of which I have only a layman's view, but I honestly think that Marilyn's the most complicated woman I've ever known. Her complexes are so complex that she even has complexes about complexes. That, I think, is one reason why she's always leaning on weird little people who attach themselves to her like remoras, and why she lets herself be guided by them. A remora is a sucker fish which attaches itself to a bigger fish and eats the dribblings which fall from the bigger fish's mouth. After she became prominent, a lot of these little people latched onto Marilyn. They told her that Hollywood was a big, greedy ogre who was exploiting her and holding back her artistic progress."

I said that the way I'd heard it, those hangers-on seemed to come and go, and that her trail was strewn with those from whom she had detached herself.

"But while they're latched onto her she has complete

61

confidence in these little odd balls, both men and women, who attach themselves to her," Jones said. "I'm sure their basic appeal to her has always been that somebody is taking advantage of her, and in some cases they've been right. This has nothing to do with your story, but it does have something to do with my observation that she's frightened and insecure, and she'll listen to anybody who can get her ear."

"Johnny Hyde was no remora," I said.

"Johnny was a switch on the usual pattern," Smith agreed. "He was devoted to her. He could and did do things for her. I happen to know that Johnny wanted to marry her and Marilyn wouldn't do it. She told me, 'I like him very much, but I don't love him enough to marry him.' A lot of girls would have married him, for Johnny was not only attractive, he was wealthy, and when he died Marilyn would have inherited scads of money, but while you may not believe it, she's never cared about money as money. It's only a symbol to her."

"A symbol of what?" I asked.

"It's my guess that to her it's a symbol of success. By the same token I think that people have talked so much to her about *not* getting what she ought to get that a *lack* of large quantities of it has also become a symbol of oppression in her mind. If I sound contradictory, that's the way it is."

I kept plugging away at it. I said to Marilyn: "You've heard it argued back and forth as to whether you are a complicated person or a very simple person, even a naïve person. Which do you think is right?"

"I've already said that I think I'm a mixture of simplicity and complexes," she told me. "But I'm beginning to understand myself now. I can face myself more, you might say. I've spent most of my life running away from myself."

It didn't sound very clear to me, so I pursued the subject further. "For example," I asked, "do you have an inferiority complex? Are you beset by fears? Do you need someone to tell you you're doing well all the time?"

"I don't feel as hopeless as I did," she said. "I don't know why it is. I've read a little of Freud and it might have to do with what he said. I think he was on the right track."

I gave up. I never found out what portions of Freud she referred to or what "right track" he was on.

"There's something I want to ask you," I said. "It's about a man in the Fox Studio legal department to whom you said, 'I don't care about money, I just want to be wonderful.' He didn't quite know what you meant by it. I must admit I'm curious myself."

"I meant that I want to be a real actress instead of a superficial actress," she said. "Now for the first time I'm learning to use myself fully as an actress. I want to add something to what I had before. Some people thought that they were getting their money's worth when they saw me in *Seven Year Itch,* but I want people to get even more for their money when they see me in the future. Only today a taxi driver said to me, 'Why did they ever put you in that little stinker, *River of No Return?* '"

"It was a good question," she said. "I'm with that taxi driver. He's my boy. Knowing what I know now, I wouldn't accept *River of No Return* today. I think that I deserve a better deal than a Z cowboy movie, in which the acting finishes second to the scenery and the Cinemascope process. The studio was Cinemascope-conscious then. That meant that it was pushing the scenery instead of pushing actors and actresses."

Milton H. Greene spoke up. "Marilyn's remark, 'I just want to be wonderful,' " he said, "meant that she wants to

63

be in the kind of pictures where she can develop; not just wear tights."

I jotted down his comment on a piece of paper so I'd remember it; then I said to Marilyn that one of the publicity men at Fox had told me that he had worked with her for several years, and that in all that time he'd never heard her tell a lie. "That's a mighty fine record for any community," I said.

"It may be a fine record," she said, "but it has also gotten me into trouble. Telling the truth, I mean. Then, when I get into trouble being too direct and I try to pull back, people think I'm coy.

"My reputation for being 'direct' is not good for me," she said. "You take what I'm supposed to have said about disliking being interviewed by women reporters, but that with gentlemen of the press it's different, because we have a mutual appreciation of being male and female. Well I didn't say that I disliked women reporters. As dumb as I am, I wouldn't be that dumb, although that in itself is kind of a mysterious remark because people don't really know how dumb I am. But I honestly prefer men reporters. They're more stimulating. That's probably why."

Without missing a beat and without a perceptible pause she switched gears into another subject. "One of the things about leaving Hollywood and coming to New York and attending the Actors' Studio is that I feel I can afford to be more myself," she said. "After all, if I can't be myself, who can I be I would like to know."

I shook my head. She had me puzzled, too.

Getting back to straight Q. and A., I told her, "I hear that you're usually late for appointments. What are the psychological reasons behind your lateness?"

64

"The Johnston Office spends a lot of time worrying about whether a girl has any cleavage or not. It seems to me that they ought to worry if she *doesn't* have any. That really would upset people.... Maybe they expect girls to look like boys." ... M.M. WITH ACE CAMERAMAN, LEON SHAMROY.   PHIL BURCHMAN

"No matter how much a person learns about being a better actress, a person isn't suddenly going to change and wear high-necked, long-sleeved dresses and dye her hair black."

PHIL BURCHMAN

"I don't know," she said. "If I knew I'd get over it. I've never come to any conclusion."

I said that I'd heard she was so nervous before appointments that she was sometimes actively nauseated. I asked her if it was caused by a feeling of pressure; of people pushing and hauling and pulling at her.

"You'd throw up too, in some situations," she told me. "For instance, I flew into New York at eight o'clock one morning and there were all those photographers waiting to take pictures of me at the airport, and all that morning I had a series of interviews with newspaper people. Those interviews came twenty minutes or a half hour apart. Then I was rushed to a luncheon with a group of magazine people, and right after luncheon I tore over to the Daily News Building. I don't think anybody can take that kind of a routine very long.

"Another complication is that I have a certain sort of stupid sincerity. I mean I don't want to tell everybody who interviews me the same thing. I want them all to have something new and different and exclusive. When I worry about that, I start to get sick at my stomach."

I asked her if writers had ever prepared material for her to use in an "interview" or in a "by-line story."

"I refuse to let articles appear in movie magazines signed, 'By Marilyn Monroe,'" she said. "I might never see that article and it might be okayed by somebody in the studio. This is wrong, because when I was a little girl I read signed stories in fan magazines and I believed every word the stars said in them. Then I'd try to model my life after the lives of the stars I read about. If I'm going to have that kind of influence, I want to be sure it's because of something I've actually said or written."

By this time Wilder's specially ground round beef on rye

toast with French fries and sliced onions arrived, and he was making ready to do away with it. Turning to him, I asked, "Why do you suppose our friend Marilyn left Hollywood the last time she checked out?"

"She's very impressionable," he told me, looking up, "and after all, many people told her that the studio was mismanaging her career. I think that at first she listened to them with one ear and then, after her bad reviews in *No Business Like Show Business,* she listened with both ears. Reviewers seem to enjoy hacking away at her. She's a favorite target for the New York critics. They find it easy to turn a funny phrase at her expense."

"Did she have any idea that she was going to lay a cake in *No Business?*" I asked.

"She was against taking that part from the very first," Flack Jones said. "She didn't want to do it, but she was forced into it; she fought against it and she hated it. In all fairness, I will say that after the studio made her do it, they did let her have her own dance director and her own dramatic coach, but even that didn't help her come off too well in the film."

On the far side of the table I heard Milton H. Greene say, "One day I plan to do a cookbook for dogs. It would contain dog-dish recipes. I think it would be amusing."

I brought him back from his dog-cookbook project to his association with Marilyn. "In Hollywood, Marilyn and I got to talking," he said. "This was after she made *Seven Year Itch* and after her divorce from Joe. I found that all Marilyn wants is to make just enough money to be able to afford to make good pictures. That's the way I feel about it too, so Marilyn Monroe Productions hopes to buy a good story property; then approach the right studio about making and distributing the picture. That's what we're

68

doing with Terence Rattigan's play, *The Sleeping Prince,* which we've bought for Marilyn's first independent venture. If the need arises, I will give up a certain amount of money and take time helping see that it is done right, settling only for what I need to live on. If Marilyn had been only interested in making money she wouldn't have been interested in me."

Thinking of Marilyn's move to New York from California, I remembered a story a producer friend of mine had told me about Marilyn's first meeting with Gregory Peck. My producer friend is also a friend of Peck's. It seemed that Peck was in New York for the sequences for *The Man in the Gray Flannel Suit.* The date happened to coincide with Judy Garland's first appearance on television, and Peck had asked a few people to drop in to his hotel suite to watch Judy.

A publicity man who worked for both Marilyn and Peck telephoned Peck and said, "I've got a date. May I bring her up?"

"Sure," Greg said.

"It's MM," the publicity man said.

Greg asked, "Who is MM?"

"Marilyn Monroe," the publicity man said, in the surprised tones of a member of the White House inner circle asked to explain the meaning of the initials D.D.E.

"Fine," Peck said. "Fetch her on over."

Presently the publicity man arrived alone, and Peck asked, "Where is MM?"

"She got tied up with some friends over in Brooklyn," the press agent said. "She'll be along later."

The guests sat down to have a look at Judy on the TV screen, and presently Marilyn came in with a couple of necktieless fellow students from the Actors' Studio. They sat down and watched the show. "After the lights were

69

switched on," my producer friend told me, "Greg asked Marilyn, 'Do you want a drink?' and she said, 'No, thank you,' then she added primly, 'I don't think we've met.'

" 'But I recognize you,' Greg said.

" 'I recognize you, too,' Marilyn said.

"It tickled Greg almost to death, but he solemnly went through a formal introduction, and everything was O.K.," my producer friend told me. "Afterwards, Marilyn disappeared with the two boys who'd brought her, and Greg asked the publicity worker with some wonderment, 'What kind of a date was that you had?'

" 'That's the way it is,' the publicity worker said vaguely.

"She didn't come with him and she didn't leave with him," my producer friend said. "The whole deal was characteristically off-beat. But Greg told me that she was pleasant enough; in fact, he thought her kind of cute.

" 'Why do you like her?' I asked him. 'Why do you think she's cute?'

" 'I don't know exactly," he said. 'But I do.' "

I said to Billy Wilder, "Although I live back in Philadelphia, I followed you vicariously through your filming of *Seven Year Itch*. I read every item I could find about that picture in the papers. As I remember it, it was along toward the end of the shooting that Marilyn and Joe DiMaggio decided to call their marriage a day, and had a parting scene in the front yard of their home with spectators hanging from the trees and photographers popping flash bulbs like fireflies."

"I think we were about halfway through when that happened," Wilder said.

"Was Joe annoyed with her because of the publication of the photos of her skirts blowing around her shoulders while she stood over a subway grating in New York for that

70

"Marilyn's first holdout was in '53 . . . when she'd finished *River of No Return*. She decided . . . that she was worth more money, but instead of prancing into Darryl Zanuck's office, slapping a script down and saying, 'I don't want to do this script!' she started hiding out." IN RIVER OF NO RETURN SHE PLINKED A GUITAR.   PHIL BURCHMAN

"If you ask me, I think I'm a mixture, of what I don't know."   PHIL BURCHMAN

"In contrast to the old Marilyn, in her present incarnation she is a liberated soul, happy, co-operative, friendly, relaxed. Actually, it is as if she had undergone a psychoanalysis so successful that the analyst himself was flabbergasted."

PHIL BURCHMAN

"Some men prefer subtleties and other men don't want things so subtle. I don't believe in false modesty. If a woman's coy she's denying herself an important part of life."

PHIL BURCHMAN

skirt-flying sequence in *Itch?*" I asked. "Some of the papers said he was."

"While I was shooting the scene Joe was standing on the sidelines," Wilder said. "I did it over and over again to get it right, and as far as I could see, Joe didn't seem irate. Anyhow, that shot didn't go as far as the famous calendar she posed for. For that matter, when you come right down to it, that calendar is not repulsive. It's quite lovely.

"Marilyn's name was already pretty big when that calendar story broke," Wilder went on. "If it hadn't been, nobody would have cared one way or the other about it. But when it became known that she had posed for it, I think it helped her popularity if anything. It appealed to people who like to read about millionaires who start off in life selling newspapers on the corner of Forty-second and Fifth Avenue; then work their way up. That pose took hours; it was as if she had been working her way through college. Here was a girl who needed dough and she made it by honest toil."

I asked Marilyn to tell me the story of that nude calendar herself, and she said, "When the studio first heard about it, everybody there was in a frenzy. They telephoned me on the set where I was working in a quickie called *Don't Bother to Knock*. The person who called asked me, 'What's all this about a calendar of you in the nude? Did you do it?'

"'Yes,' I said. 'Is there anything wrong with that? So they've found out it's me on that calendar! Well, what do you know!'

"'Found out!' he almost screamed. 'There you are, all of you, in full color!' Then he must have gotten mixed up, for first he said, 'Just deny everything'; then he said, 'Don't say anything. I'll be right down.'

"I was working on the Fox Western Avenue lot when this worried man from Fox came tearing in wringing his hands,"

73

Marilyn told me. "He took me into my dressing room to talk about the dreadful thing I'd done in posing for such a photograph. I could think of nothing else to say, so I said apologetically, 'I thought the lighting the photographer used would disguise me.' I thought that man would have a stroke when I said that."

"What had happened was that I was behind in my rent at the Hollywood Studio Club, where girls live who hope to crash the movies. You're only supposed to get one week behind in your rent at the club, but they must have felt sorry for me because they'd given me three warnings. A lot of photographers had asked me to pose in the nude, but I'd always said, 'No.' I was getting five dollars an hour for plain modeling, but the price for nude modeling was fifty an hour. So I called Tom Kelley, a photographer I knew, and said, 'They're kicking me out of here. How soon can we do it?' He said, 'We can do it tomorrow.'

"I didn't even have to get dressed, so it didn't take long. I mean it takes longer to get dressed than it does to get undressed. I'd asked Tom, 'Please don't have anyone else there except your wife, Natalie.' He said, 'O.K.' He only made two poses. There was a shot of me sitting up and a shot of me lying down. I think the one of me lying down is the best."

Marilyn said that after the alarmed person from the studio scurried out of her dressing room, the next thing she knew she was having luncheon with a writer from the United Press. Marilyn told the writer about the calendar, and that afternoon there was a calendar story in the Los Angeles *Herald*. For a while there was a stunned silence from the Fox front office. "Then they decided to put out the facts with no apologies," Marilyn told me. "Maybe they figured that that reporter would regard her luncheon with

74

me as being off the record, but I never told her that I thought it was."

I asked Marilyn if she was surprised when the news of the calendar got out.

"Not exactly," she said. "Just before I went back to Fox to work in *Don't Bother to Knock*, I'd been at RKO on a loan-out, working in a picture called *Clash by Night*. While I was at RKO, mysterious people kept calling up Jerry Wald, who was in charge of production there, and trying to blackmail him by saying they were going to break a story about me having posed in the nude for a calendar, and that news like that would put the kiss of death on *Clash by Night* if Mr. Wald didn't do thus and so for them."

Flack Jones broke in to say, "That calendar will probably be reprinted as long as we have men with twenty-twenty vision in this country."

"I'm saving a copy of it for my grandchildren," Marilyn went on, bright-eyed. "There's a place in Los Angeles which even reproduces it on bras or panties. But I have only autographed a few copies of it, mostly for sick people. And I signed one for the cameraman on the picture in which I was working when the calendar story broke. On one I wrote, 'This may not be my best angle,' and on another I wrote, 'Do you like me better with long hair?'"

To double-check, I asked, "Do you think men like their sex subtle or fairly obvious?" I already had the male answer from Flack Jones.

It seemed to me that she hedged a little. "Some men prefer subtleties and other men don't want things so subtle," she said. "I don't believe in false modesty. A woman only hurts herself that way. If she's coy she's denying herself an important part of life. Men sometimes believe that you're frigid and cold in the development of a relationship, but if

75

they do, it's not always their fault. Religion has to do with it and how you're brought up. You're stuck with all those things."

Behind us, just over a white brick wall, a bevy of the members of the Beverly Hills Junior League chattered their way into the small oval clubhouse they occupied there. They chattered in light, airy tones. Their hats looked as colorful as birds' crests. For some reason they made me think of another episode out of Marilyn's life — perhaps because they were so remote from it.

"What happened in 1952, when the studio sent you to Atlantic City to be grand marshal of the annual beauty pageant?" I asked Marilyn. "Did you mind going?"

She smiled. "It was all right with me," she said. "At the time I wanted to come to New York anyhow because there was somebody I wanted to see there. That's why it was hard for me to be on time leaving New York for Atlantic City for that date. I missed the train and the studio chartered a plane for me, but that didn't set the studio back as much money as they let on. They could afford it."

Flack Jones took up the story at that point. "They'd arranged a big reception for Marilyn at Atlantic City," he told me. "They had a band to meet her at the train, and the mayor was to be on hand. Marilyn and the flacks who were running interference for her were to arrive on a Pennsylvania Railroad train at a certain hour, but, as usual, Marilyn was late, and when they got to the Pennsylvania Station the train had pulled out. So there they were, in New York, with a band and the mayor waiting in Atlantic City. Charlie Einfeld, a Fox vice-president — who can operate mighty fast and efficient when the need arises — got on the phone, chartered an air liner — the only one available for

76

charter was a forty-six-seat job; it was an Eastern Air Lines plane, as I recall it — and we went screaming across town in a limousine headed for Idlewild."

"That must have taken you a good forty-five minutes," I said.

"It did," Flack Jones said. "All of that. Bob Flysher, the studio's magazine man in New York, Marilyn, and a flack from the studio boarded the plane and took off for Atlantic City. Bob and the Coast flack were embarrassed at missing the train, and the plane was such a costly substitute that they were sweating like pigs. On this big air liner there was a steward aboard — they'd shanghaied a steward in a hurry from someplace to serve coffee — but all of this didn't bother Marilyn at all. She tucked herself into a seat in the tail section, hummed softly; then fell fast asleep and slept all the way. The others sat up front with the steward, drinking quarts of coffee because that was what he was being paid to serve. They drank an awful lot of coffee."

Flack Jones said that Marilyn and her group were met at the Atlantic City Airport by a sheriff's car and that they were only three minutes late for the reception for Marilyn on the boardwalk. There she was given an enormous bouquet of flowers, and she perched on the folded-down top of a convertible, to roll down the boardwalk with a press of people following her car.

"She sat up there like Lindbergh riding down Broadway on his return from Paris," Flack Jones said. "The people and the cops and the beauty-carnival press agents and the rest followed behind like slaves tied to her chariot wheels. That is, she managed to move a little every once in a while when the crowd could be persuaded to back away. Then Marilyn would pitch a rose at them and that would set

77

them off again, and there'd be another riot. This sort of thing went on — with variations — for several days. It was frantic.

"But," Flack Jones said, "there was one publicity thing which broke which wasn't intended to break. It was typical of the way things happen to Marilyn without anybody planning them. When each potential Miss America from a different part of the country lined up to register, a photograph of Marilyn greeting her was taken. Those pictures were serviced back to the local papers and eventually a shot of Miss Colorado with Marilyn wound up in a Denver paper; a shot of Miss California and Marilyn in the Los Angeles and San Francisco papers, and so forth."

Flack Jones collected a few crumbs from the flaky crust of a hard roll, popped them into his mouth, collected his thoughts for a moment to marshal them in orderly array; then went on, "Pretty soon in came an Army public-information officer with four young ladies from the Pentagon. There was a WAF and a WAC and a lady Marine and a WAVE. The thought was that it would be nice to get a shot of Marilyn with 'the four real Miss Americas' who were serving their country, so we lined them up. It was to be just another of the routine, catalogue shots we'd taken all day long, but Marilyn was wearing a low-cut dress which showed quite a bit of cleavage — quite a bit of cleavage in fact. That would have been all right, since the dress was designed for eye level — see level, I almost said — but one of the photographers climbed up on a chair to shoot the picture."

"I had met the girls from each state and had shaken hands with them," Marilyn said. "Then this Army man got the idea of aiming his camera down my neck while I posed with the service girls. It wasn't *my* idea for the photographer to get up on a chair."

78

"She does two things beautifully. She walks and she stands still. In addition she has wit enough to buy her clothes one or two sizes too small for her. With a chassis like hers, this infuriates women and intrigues guys." . . . Danny Kaye with M.M. at a hospital benefit. PHIL BURCHMAN

". . . but so far the lines the public really wants from her are not written in English." . . . M.M. with Jane ("Can that be muscle?") Russell, in a shot from *Gentlemen Prefer Blondes*.

PHIL BURCHMAN

"Jane Russell and I were asked to put our footprints in wet concrete in front of Grauman's Chinese Theater, along with the dent left by Jimmy Durante's nose and the print of one of Betty Grable's legs. I suggested that Jane lean over the wet cement and that I sit in it."

PHIL BURCHMAN

Flack Jones resumed his story, "Nobody thought anything of it at the time," he said, "and those around Marilyn went on with the business of their workaday world. In due course the United Press — among others — serviced that shot. Actually it was a pretty dull picture because, to the casual glance, it just showed five gals lined up looking at the camera."

Jones said that when the shot of the four service women and Marilyn went out across the country by wirephoto, editors took one look at it and dropped it into the nearest wastebasket because they had much better art from Atlantic City.

"That night the Army PIO officer drifted back to the improvised press headquarters they set up for the Miss America contest," Flack Jones said. "He took one look and sent out a wire ordering that the picture be stopped."

"On what grounds?" I asked.

"On grounds that that photograph showed too much meat and potatoes, and before he'd left the Pentagon he'd been told not to have any cheesecake shots taken in connection with the girls in his charge. Obviously what was meant by those instructions was that they shouldn't have those service girls sitting on the boardwalk railings showing their legs or assuming other undignified poses. There was nothing in that PIO officer's instructions which gave him the right to censor Marilyn's garb, but he ordered that picture killed anyhow."

According to Jones, every editor who'd junked that picture immediately reached down into his wastebasket, drew it out, and gave it a big play. "In Los Angeles it ran seven columns," he said, "and it got a featured position in the *Herald Express* and in the New York *Daily News*. All the way across country it became a celebrated picture, and all because the Army had 'killed' it."

81

He was silent for a moment; looking through the greenery at the new wing of the hotel as if he expected to see scenes from the past reflected there as on a movie screen. "Those who were with her told me afterward that it had been a murderous day, as any day is when you're with Marilyn on a junket," he went on. "The demands on her and on those with her are simply unbelievable. But finally she hit the sack about midnight because she had to get up the next day for other activities. The rest of her crowd had turned in too, when they got a call from the U.P. in New York, asking them for a statement from Marilyn about 'that picture.'"

Flack Jones pressed a forefinger on the table top until its nail turned white. He flexed his thumb and went on. " 'What picture?' her publicist guardian asked. "It was then that they got the story. They hated to do it, but they rousted Marilyn out of bed. She thought it over for a while; then issued a statement apologizing for any possible reflection on the service girls, and making it plain that she hadn't meant it that way. She ended with a genuine Monroeism. 'I wasn't aware of any objectionable *décolletage* on my part. I'd noticed people looking at me all day, but I thought they were looking at my grand marshal's badge.' This was widely quoted, and it had the effect of giving the whole thing a lighter touch.

"Turnabout is fair play," Flack Jones said, "and the next day somebody with authority in the Pentagon issued a sort of apology in which they said they had meant no offense to Miss Monroe. But the point is this: a lot of things happen when Marilyn is around." He shook his head. "Yes, sir," he said. "A lot of things."

I asked Marilyn what she thought of the phase through which Hollywood had gone in which it had tried to publicize its glamorous feminine stars with picture layouts showing them as "the cake-baking girl next door" or as "homebody, slippers-and-fireside types."

"The whole thing is too ridiculous," she said. "I wouldn't let any magazine in to photograph the little things I do around the house. They wouldn't be interested anyhow but I can assure you that I am not baking cakes."

"Another example of the impact she packs," Jones went on, "was when she went back to New York on *The Seven Year Itch* location." All of a sudden New York was a whistle stop, with the folks all down to see the daily train come in. When Marilyn reached LaGuardia, everything stopped out there. One columnist remarked that the Russians could have buzzed the field at five hundred feet and nobody would have looked up. There has seldom been such a heavy concentration of newsreel cameramen anywhere. From then on in, during the ten days of her stay, one excitement followed another. She was on the front page of the *Herald Tribune*, with art, five days running, which I was told set some sort of a local record.

"Things reached a new high — and no joke intended," Flack Jones went on, "when Billy Wilder shot the scene where her skirts were swept up around her shoulders by a draft from a subway ventilator grating. That really set the publicity afire again, and shortly after that they blew town while they were ahead. The unit production manager had picked the Trans-Lux Theater on Lexington Avenue for the skirt-blowing scene. He'd been down there at two o'clock in the morning to case the spot; he'd reported happily, 'The street was fully deserted,' and he'd made a deal with the Trans-Lux people for getting the scene shot there because there was nobody on the street at that hour.

"It seemed certain that Billy Wilder would have all the room in the world to work, and he had left word that nobody was to know what location he'd selected, because he didn't want crowds. But the news leaked out. It was on radio and TV and in the papers, so instead of secrecy you might almost say that the public was being urged to be at Lexington Avenue on a given night to watch Marilyn's skirts blow. So instead of having a nice, quiet side street in which to work, Wilder had all the people you can pack on a street. Finally the cops roped off the sidewalk on the opposite side to restrain the public, and they erected a barricade close to the camera. But that wasn't good enough, and they had to call out a whole bunch of special cops."

Flack Jones said that when Wilder was ready to shoot, there were 200 or 300 photographers, professional and amateur, swarming all over the place. Then Marilyn made her entrance from inside the theater out onto the sidewalk, and when she appeared the hordes really got out of control. There was chaos. Finally Wilder announced that he'd enter into a gentleman's agreement. If the press would retire behind the barricades, and if the real working photographers would help control the amateurs, he would shoot the scene of Marilyn standing with Tom Ewell over the subway grating; then he'd move the movie camera back and the amateur shutter hounds could pop away at Marilyn until they were satisfied. So the New York press took care of the amateurs and made them quit popping their flash bulbs for the time being. Wilder got the scene and the volunteer snapshots got their pictures.

"Everybody was there," Flack Jones went on. "Including DiMaggio. To me he showed a husbandly disapproval of the proceedings. Myself I couldn't see why Joe disapproved. After all, when he married the girl her figure was already highly publicized, and it would seem odd if he suddenly decided that she should be seen only in Mother Hubbards."

"For a man and a wife to live intimately together is no easy thing at best. If it's not just exactly right in every way it's practically impossible. However, I'm still optimistic."   PHIL BURCHMAN

"When that romance reached full flower, the studio had to do a fast switcheroo. There we were, issuing communiqués about this 'silly, stubborn little dame who was ill-advised enough not to come back and take this important part' in whatever the picture was — *Pink Tights* — when all of a sudden she ups and marries Joe, the All-American Boy."

PHIL BURCHMAN

"People say it's chic to have separate bedrooms. . . . With a separate bedroom deal, if you think of something you want to say to the other one, you have to go traipsing down the hall. . . . You may forget what you started out to say." M.M. on her honeymoon with her (and the American League's) Prince Charming.

PHIL BURCHMAN

I asked Marilyn herself whether she thought that Joe had disapproved of her skirts blowing up around her shoulders. I said that I had heard his reaction described in two ways: that he had been irritated and that he had taken it calmly.

"One of those two is correct," Marilyn said. "If you'll give it a little thought maybe you can figure it out for yourself."

Something told me that, in her opinion, Joe had been very annoyed indeed.

I guided the conversation to a story I'd read, written by Aline Mosby of the United Press. The story was to the effect that Marilyn had once told her that she had bought Joe a king-size, eight-foot bed because she didn't approve of separate bedrooms.

"People say it's very chic to have separate bedrooms," Marilyn told me. "That way a man can have a place for his fishing equipment and guns as well as for sleeping, and a woman can have a fluffy, ruffly place with rows of perfume bottles clinking against each other. But the way I feel, they ought to share the same bedroom. With a separate bedroom deal, if you happen to think of something you want to say to the other one, it means you have to go traipsing down the hall, and you may be tired. For that matter, you may forget what you started out to say. Besides, separate bedrooms are lonely. I think people need human warmth even when they're asleep and unconscious.

"For a man and a wife to live intimately together is no easy thing at best," she went on. "If it's not just exactly right in every way it's practically impossible. However, I'm still optimistic."

She sat there being optimistic. Then she said, with feeling, "However, I think TV sets should be taken out of the bedroom."

87

"Did you and Joe have one in your bedroom?" I asked.

She said emphatically, "No comment. But everything I say to you I speak from experience. You can make what you want of that."

"At any event, that location trip to New York was a break for the columnist Earl Wilson," Flack Jones broke in. "Earl, who is a well-known opponent of flat chests, brought Gina Lollobrigida over to see the New York *Seven Year Itch* shooting, and he got a shot of himself between Marilyn and Gina. It made a very cute setting. By coincidence, both of the girls were wearing plunging-neckline, halter-top, pleated white dresses, and there was no need for any caption writer to say, 'This one in the middle is Wilson.'

"Earl's wife thought faster than Earl. After Lolo was shot with Earl and Marilyn. Mrs. Wilson suggested to Lolo that she was tired and that she ought to go back to her hotel, so she disappeared before the rest of the press knew she was there. The result was that almost the only available shot of those two sex balls together shows Earl between them."

Flack Jones ran his fingers over his head of skin and said, "In the case of *The Seven Year Itch,* there was a contractual-restriction situation. The studio's contract called for the picture's release to be held up until after the Broadway run of the play.

"When Marilyn went back to New York for the location shots for *Itch,* the play version was still doing a fair business, but it was approaching the end of its long run. If you bought a seat, the house was only half full. Then Marilyn arrived in New York and publicity sparks shot off and suddenly the *Itch* had S.R.O. signs out front again. As a result it seemed that it was never going to stop its stage run; so, after finishing the picture, Fox had to pay out an additional hundred

88

and seventy-five thousand dollars to the owners of the stage property for the privilege of releasing their movie."

Flack Jones poured fresh coffee. "Marilyn's first holdout was in late '52," he said. "No, come to think of it, it must have been '53, for she'd finished *How to Marry a Millionaire* and *River of No Return.* She decided (or rather, her confidential advisers had persuaded her) that she was worth more money, but instead of prancing into Darryl Zanuck's office, slapping a script down, and saying, 'I don't want to do this script!' she started hiding out."

"Wasn't what she did a new deal in holdouts?" I asked.

"You could call it that," Flack Jones said. "She couldn't be reached by anybody. There she was sneaking around in alleys, and not answering her phone. We will refer to this as Holdout Number One, the one before she ran off and married Joe DiMaggio.

"When that romance reached full flower, the studio had to do a fast switcheroo. There we were, issuing communiqués about this 'silly, stubborn little dame who was ill-advised enough not to come back and take this important part' in whatever the picture was — *Pink Tights,* I think — when all of a sudden she ups and marries Joe, the All-American Boy. After that, if we kept on beefing and squawking about her absence, the studio would become the heavy in the plot so far as the public was concerned."

"When did Joe come into her life?" I asked.

"She had a blind double date one night, and met him in a café," Jones told me. "Marilyn was making a picture, and DiMaggio had heard about her and wanted to meet her. They met through friends and had dinner. Everything went fine, until their friendship built up into a romance which led to marriage."

I asked her if she and DiMaggio had taken two years to

89

decide to be married. I'd heard that their courtship had lasted that long.

"We weren't spending those two years deciding to get married," she said. "When it happened it was sudden."

"Then, to add to the studio's confusion," Flack Jones continued, "the pair went off to Korea to entertain the troops. How are you going to snap a black snake whip around a girl's calves after a thing like that? Snow White has married Prince Charming and they've gone to Korea together to entertain the troops, so the studio started talking sweet in a hurry."

Rhubarb, the Beverly Hills Loggia cat, stalked slowly past, intent on his own affairs. He looked to neither the left nor the right.

"You could tell that that marriage was in danger as early as their arrival in the Orient," Flack Jones said. "In Tokyo the press interviewed Marilyn and a story with a Tokyo date line came back to the states which said they had talked to Marilyn Monroe about this and about that, and the release went on to say that there was a forgotten man in the far corner of the room whose name was Joe DiMaggio. It didn't take much of a genius to figure that as the beginning of the end. Then, after a while the lovebirds flew back to Beverly Hills."

"Did the studio start having its troubles making her report for work before she married DiMaggio or after she married him?" I asked.

"We were having trouble before," Flack Jones said.

"When was the first rift in the Monroe-Fox lute?" I asked.

"I don't know the exact time," he said. "But the timing was not peculiar to Monroe. It's peculiar to life in Hollywood. It's what almost invariably happens when money and success make an impact on the male or female ego there.

90

"You fellows down there are always whistling at sweater girls. Well, take away their sweaters and what have you got?"

WHY DID SHE BLOW HER MARRIAGE WITH JOE DIMAGGIO? WHY DID SHE WALK OUT ON A MOVIE CAREER THAT WAS PAYING HER HEAVY MONEY? WHY DID SHE ATTEND THE ACTORS' STUDIO — SURELY AN UNLIKELY PLACE OR A GIRL WHO, UP TO THAT TIME, WAS SUPPOSED TO HAVE DONE MOST OF HER ACTING WITH HER HIPS?

PHIL BURCHMAN

You expect it to set in when the fan mail of the party in question zooms up to over two thousand a week. It's almost as much of a sure thing as the thermostat in your house turning on the heat. Two thousand fan letters a week is when we begin to say, 'It won't be long now. We'll soon be having troubles with this doll.' "

"What form does it usually take?" I asked. " 'I want more dough' or 'I don't like my contract' or 'I think my next script stinks'?"

"Perhaps a better way to answer your question is to say that when they realize they've got weight to throw around, they begin to throw it," Flack Jones declared. "They don't do those other things you mentioned right away; they do the less serious things first. They complain about wardrobe, or, if it's a musical, they complain about the songs or the dances; or if it's a plain comedy or a straight drama, they beef about how a certain scene is being directed. Whatever's handy, that's what they complain about. It makes no sense, but it's a means of highlighting the fact that now that they *do* have some weight they want you to know it."

"What's the next move?" I asked.

Flack Jones did the fingers-over-his-scalp bit again and said, "Ordinarily it's a test of strength, like bracing the front office for more dough for your dramatic coach. Marilyn did that for her drama coach, and everyone said, 'Isn't she wonderful? Here's a girl going all out to help a person who's not as big as she is.' It shows that she has a good, fine, wonderful heart. She's interested in everyone's welfare except her own.

"Remember," Jones said, "from now on what I say is merely my own opinion, but I think that when she found out she had that much weight, she decided to go out for herself, and she did. Most people think that this is a naïve,

93

flibbertigibbet girl moving through life. This is utter nonsense. She wasn't that way when she first was under contract; she was a grown person. She kept her dates, she was always on time. Then she discovered that a segment of Hollywood respects people who kick its teeth in. For that matter, a lot of people do. Not just Hollywood. Anyplace."

Rex handed around menus so that we could select our dessert. He lured only two customers. I ordered Mr. Courtright's cookies and Flack Jones said he'd like *flambé au rhum*.

"Let's cut to the split-up between Joe and Marilyn," I said. "As I remember it, first there were rumors of strife; then things reached an impasse."

"The final scenes of All-American Boy loses Snow White were unbelievable," Flack Jones told me. "Joe and Marilyn had a rented house on Palm Drive, in Beverly Hills, and we had a unique situation there with the embattled ex-lovebirds both cooped in the same cage. Marilyn was living on the second floor and Joe was camping on the first floor. Then the nationally famed attorney, Jerry Giesler, was brought into the act as Marilyn's mouthpiece, although why they had to employ such a great lawyer to handle a simple divorce case I don't know. The public is all worked up, and the press is too, and together they're circling that house on Palm Drive like Indians loping around a wagon train, waiting for somebody to poke his head out. The next move was Giesler's announcement that come Wednesday, at eleven o'clock, Marilyn would hold a press conference in his office."

I found myself hoping that no one would call Flack Jones on one of the Loggia's portable telephones. He was going strong. I didn't want him interrupted.

"In the Fox publicity department, it was concluded that

94

if you call a press conference in a lawyer's office," he said, "it presupposes an obligation on your part to say something, and if there's anybody in the world who was in no position to say anything about anything, it was Marilyn. I mean, what could Snow White say when she was breaking up with Prince Charming, or Cinderella say when she was phffting from the All-American Boy.

"Any press conference announcement was only going to bring more characters out to chase Marilyn from her house to Giesler's office. And once they got there, if anybody issued one of those 'it's just one of those things; a couple of young people who couldn't make a go of it' statements, it was only going to irritate everybody.

"So the studio issued a statement in advance. It said that Marilyn wasn't going to make any press statements and that there'd be no interview, but that she'd be leaving for work at ten o'clock from her house, to fulfill her commitment on *Seven Year Itch,* based on the Broadway play of the same name and costarring Tom Ewell, in Cinemascope.

"Once we'd gotten that plug in, we said that while we didn't promise an interview, the boys would get some pictures. So forty or fifty of the press congregated. In addition, there were several hundred volunteer reporters and photographers up in the trees and tramping down the lawn.

"Then the greatest thing in the world happened," Flack Jones said. He grinned when the thought of it. "They were all there to get a picture of Marilyn going to work, because it would be the first picture since her announcement that she wanted a divorce, and on top of that, Joe's inside, too. So there was a lot of coming and going. Among the early comers was a hairdresser and a make-up man because Marilyn had to be ready to go to work. Her lawyer went in and there was a lot of whispering, all of which built up suspense."

95

Jones went on, "All at once, in front of the house a great, big, beautiful automobile pulled up. In it was a friend of Joe's from San Francisco. As I've said, Joe's been in that house for three days on the first floor, with Marilyn on the second. There was a back alley, and a rejected husband could have snuck out of that back alley and disappeared if he'd wanted to. But the All-American Boy faced up to his responsibilities and took them like a man. So, what do the press and the newsreels get? A bonus! Out of the front door comes Joe, grim-lipped, walking the last mile, with his pal carrying his suitcase.

"The press stopped him on the lawn, but Joe had no comment to make. They got pictures of him as he climbed into the car, holding it long enough for one guy to ask, 'Where you going, Joe?'

" 'I'm going home,' Joe said.

" 'We thought this was your home, Joe,' the press chirped like a Greek chorus.

" 'San Francisco has always been my home,' Joe said.

"He stood there waving farewell until everybody had a shot; then he drove away."

Looking at Flack Jones's face, I could see that he was still reliving a scene no press agent could have invented in his wildest dreams. "When Joe walked out of that first floor, it was like the heart-tearing business of a pitcher taking the long trudge from the mound to the dugout after being jerked from the game in a World Series," he said. "I've always admired Joe for that. A lot of guys with less courage would have sneaked out the back way and would have scampered off to San Francisco, by-passing that encounter in the front yard. Not old Joe.

"Then, about ten minutes later, Marilyn came down the stairs sobbing, on Jerry Giesler's arm. She was all broken

96

"To add to the studio's confusion, the pair went off to Korea. How are you going to snap a black snake whip around a girl's calves after a thing like that? Snow White has married Prince Charming and they've gone to entertain the troops, so the studio started talking sweet." PHIL BURCHMAN

"One reason why she's such a good interview is that she uses her head. She tries to say something that's amusing and quotable, and she usually does." PHIL BURCHMAN

up. She'd spent three sleepless nights, during which she'd been almost constantly sick at her stomach. Everybody was shoving and pushing, and a lady columnist kicked the crime reporter for the Los Angeles *Mirror* on the shins.

"He turned to her and asked, 'Who do you think you're kicking?' and she said, 'I'll kick you in the pants if you don't get out of my way.'

"All in all, there was quite a hubbub. The newsreel guys were grinding and somebody asked, 'How about Joe, Marilyn?' and Marilyn said, between sobs, 'I can't talk. I can't!' Finally she reached her lawyer's car and drove off."

There was quiet around our table for a moment in the Beverly Hills Hotel Loggia; then Marilyn said, "When I showed up in divorce court, there were mobs of people there asking me bunches of questions. They asked, 'Are you and Joe still friends?' I said, 'Yes, but I still don't know anything about baseball.' And they all laughed. I don't see what was funny. I'd heard that he was a fine baseball player, but I'd never seen him play."

Flack Jones said nothing for a moment, then he picked up the conversational threads and began to splice them together once more. "She came back and finished *Itch* at Fox," he said. "Then her agent, Charlie Feldman, flung a snazzy party for her at Romanoff's. After that she went to New York and didn't come back.

"But before she blew town, she buttonholed Darryl Zanuck at some affair. He'd only met her twice before, but she said to him that she didn't like the title of the picture the studio was cooking up for her, *How to Be Very, Very Popular* or *The Girl in the Red Velvet Swing* or something like that. 'You know, the title is very important,' she told him. Zanuck has only been in the movie business about thirty years and he knows a little about titles himself, so

99

this remark of Marilyn's kind of threw him. All he could say was, 'Well I'll be jiggered!' only that wasn't quite what he said.

"The next thing anybody knew she announced that she had formed Marilyn Monroe, Inc., with Milton Green as vice-president. But I have reason to think that she had done that before she left Hollywood, for a hairdresser at the studio told me that one day, when he had Marilyn in front of his mirror, she had said, 'Gee, I feel good. I'm incorporated!' "

"I'm not too clear on this," I said. "When she left the studio that last time, was it a clean, sharp break or did her relations with the studio gradually become fuzzy and vague until finally there weren't any relations left?"

"She simply didn't show up again after *Seven Year Itch*," Flack Jones said. "I don't know whether you'd call that sharp or vague."

Marilyn herself entered the conversation once more. She said, "Recently somebody asked me, 'What are you really trying to do in New York? What do you honestly want to be?'

"I told them, 'I want to be an artist. And they asked, 'You mean you want to paint, too?' It never seemed to occur to them that I want to be an artist in the theater."

I said to her, "Billy Wilder says there's no reason why you shouldn't play Grushenka in *The Brothers Karamazov* if you want to. He told me it's your kind of role. He said Grushenka is a sex pot."

"She's a lot more than that," Marilyn said. "In the story she grows and develops because of her love for a man. Billy Wilder is not the only one who believes I can play her. I read in a newspaper that Sam Goldwyn thought I could

100

play her too. Mr. Goldwyn wanted me to play Adelaide in *Guys and Dolls,* but Fox wouldn't let me."

"The way I get it," I told her, "you invented a new system of holding out. If you didn't like a role or script, you just disappeared."

"I disappeared because if people won't listen to you, there's no point in talking to people," she told me. "If they won't listen you're just banging your head against a wall. If you can't do what they want you to do, the thing is to leave. I never got a chance to learn anything in Hollywood. They worked me too fast. They rushed me from one picture into another.

"And I know who started all of those stories which were sent out about me after I left Hollywood the last time," she added. "A big studio has much power with certain columnists, and with trade papers. One paper had an editorial about me that went something like this: 'Marilyn Monroe is a very stupid girl to give up all the wonderful things the movie industry has done for her and go back to New York, hoping to learn to act!'

"Those weren't the exact words of that editorial, but that was the idea. Well, if it was supposed to scare me, it didn't. When I read it and I realized that it wasn't frightening me, I felt strong. That's why I know I'm stronger than I was. That editorial went on to say that I had been dropped by two major studios and it asked where would I have been without one of them. The writer forgot to mention that studio was one of the studios which had dropped me."

She thought that over for a while, then said, "I'm for the individual as opposed to the corporation. The way it is the individual is the underdog, and with all the things a corporation has going for them an individual comes out banged on her head. The artist is nothing. It's really tragic.

"But getting back to what you call my holdout, one of the reasons why I disappeared was that in Hollywood if a girl is unhappy about a script, she can't sit down and discuss that script with a producer. Once you say one word to the producer about it, you're legally involved in making that picture. You can be sued if you don't go through with it. If you even so much as go for a wardrobe fitting you're trapped, and they can send you a wire to report for shooting. So if you can't talk to them, so what? All that's left is to leave."

"The thing to remember," Billy Wilder told me, "and I think it's important — is that she's working in the right direction. She wants to learn and I honestly believe she's terribly sincere."

When I asked Marilyn to tell me of her association with the Actors' Studio, she said that she not only attended the regular classes there, but also the private classes taught by Lee Strasberg and his wife, who ran the Studio.

"You do scenes," she told me, "and anyone is privileged to criticize. So far I'm less shy on the stage than I've ever been in front of a camera, I have less trouble remembering my lines."

Milton H. Greene spoke up. "Marlon Brando, Jimmy Dean, Kim Stanley, Julie Harris, and Montgomery Clift all studied under the Strasbergs," he said. "Marilyn observes, studies, and watches. She listens to lectures. Occasionally she is allowed to take part."

I had been told this about the Actors' Studio. It lets interested people like Marilyn sit in on an informal, guest basis. She is not an officially enrolled student member of the Actors' Studio, because you are not admitted there on that basis unless you have contributed something notable

"Some people thought that they were getting their money's worth when they saw me in *Seven Year Itch*." PHIL BURCHMAN

"If there's anything wrong with the way American men look at sex, it's not their fault. After all, they're descended from Puritans, who got off the boat on the wrong foot — or was it the Pilgrims?" Gina Lollobrigida visits the location set for *The Seven Year Itch,* in New York City.

PHIL BURCHMAN

on the stage in a performance or have passed a series of exacting auditions. Just wanting to be in isn't enough. This is very smart of the Strasbergs, because it eliminates all those who are without talent; otherwise the studio would be full of women all seven feet tall and all trying to be actresses.

I told Marilyn that I had heard that the Associated Press had estimated that her latest contract, scheduled to run for seven years, would bring her around eight million dollars during that period. When I mentioned this, she said, "I don't know about that eight million dollars. That is a lot of money, but I am free to make as many pictures for my own company as I do for Fox and maybe with percentage deals and all, I'll make a lot; maybe I'll make less. But no matter what they tell you, it's not just for money that I'm going back to Hollywood."

"I don't know where they got that eight-million figure either," Milton H. Greene said. "Not from me and not from Marilyn. Not that they haven't been after us for a figure. Everybody wants an exclusive release or an exclusive interview with Marilyn.

"I want everybody to be happy," he went on, "but I don't ask you what *you* make, do I? Things like that are confidential between Fox and Marilyn Monroe Productions, and after all we have to work with people like Fox.

"Marilyn and I teamed up to supply the dough for Marilyn Monroe Productions," Milton H. Greene said. "Marilyn had saved up a nest egg. There are only two voting stockholders, Marilyn and I, and four directors."

My friend the producer, the one who had told me about Marilyn's first meeting with Greg Peck, had also told me: "My guess is that somebody — some man or organization with money — invested in her when she left Fox the last

105

time. It wouldn't have been too long a gamble at that. Suppose, after examining the situation with a lawyer's help, that man or that organization decided that eventually she'd be a free agent. A deal could be made with her in which she would be paid, say, a thousand dollars a week, contingent upon the fact that when she became a free agent, the investor would have certain rights in a picture or pictures she would make. Under the income-tax ruling, that would be a valid investment. If the idea flopped, what did the man or the organization stand to lose? Only the investment involved, and investment losses are deductible. Anyhow, that's my guess, because when Marilyn left Hollywood, she didn't seem to be rolling in dough."

When I complained that the press releases concerning Marilyn's new contract had seemed sketchy and uninformative and composed of double talk, my producer friend told me, "As I understand it, in place of the remainder of Marilyn's contract with Twentieth Century-Fox, which had about two and a half years to go, that studio has officially recognized the existence of Marilyn Monroe Productions and has made a contract with it for Marilyn's services."

"What's Fox going to get out of it?" I asked.

"It seems to be specified that this new contract with Marilyn Monroe Productions calls for the use of Marilyn in four pictures over a period of seven years," my producer friend said. "She is otherwise free to make her own deals for pictures elsewhere, subject to the arrangement that the first picture will be for Fox. Thereafter Fox's pictures will alternate with any others she does."

"What's in it for Marilyn, or rather, Marilyn Monroe Productions?" I asked.

"Marilyn got one hundred thousand dollars a picture for her last two at Fox, and I am told that she will do these four

106

"I don't care about money. I just want to be wonderful."   TOPIX

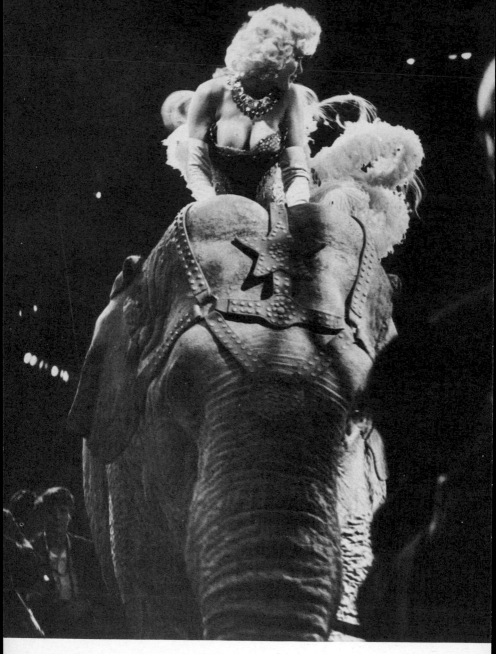

"Sex is a part of nature. I go along with nature." PHOTO-REPRESENTATIVES

future pictures at the same rate," my producer informant said. "No percentages over and above that. The studio seems satisfied with this new deal. As things were going, Marilyn could have sat out the remaining two and a half years of her existing contract and done nobody any good. As it is, the studio is assured of four pictures from her at a not unreasonable price. As for Marilyn, she gets her own corporation and the freedom to make other pictures at whatever price she can get. She is also free to do TV, stage, or night-club work."

I said I figured that she'd been holding out for special concessions of one kind or another.

His final words to me were, "She gets no story or cast approval, but Fox and Marilyn Monroe Productions have agreed on a list of about nineteen directors, any one of whom will be acceptable to both parties. In other words, if Fox submits a story to her with the name of one of these directors, she is contractually bound to do that picture, and no arguing. This does not exclude the use of some other director, assuming that both parties agree on another person who is not on the list of the magical nineteen."

A tall, gaunt, middle-aged figure passed by our table on his way out of the Polo Patio. When I saw him I thought, *He'll know the details of her old contract, as well as of her new one. He knows everything and everybody in Hollywood.* The tall, thin figure was Billy Wilkerson. He owns *The Hollywood Reporter,* a trade paper that daily publishes a digest of motion-picture, radio, and television activities.

"How about telling me about the wash-up of the old Twentieth Century-Fox-Marilyn Monroe deal and its replacement by a new go-round," I asked him.

Wilkerson paused in mid-stride and said, "It was a good

deal for Fox, since they couldn't expect to get more than four pictures during the two and one half years which remained on Monroe's old contract. It was a good deal for Monroe, too, because immediately after she finishes *Bus Stop* for Twentieth, which is her first film under her new contract, she can enter into independent deals in which she can make from two hundred thousand to one million dollars a picture — *if* the picture hits. I understand that she's now asking — or rather, that her askers are asking for her — fifty-per-cent participation rights in the profits, with a guarantee of at least two hundred thousand dollars for her services rendered to studios other than Fox."

I thanked Wilkerson and he joined friends at another table.

"Director approval is very important," Milton H. Greene said. "A great deal is in a director's hands; for example, creative ability. The right director can put a lot more into a picture than the words on the script he's given to shoot. Look what Hitchcock did with *To Catch a Thief* and what Josh Logan did with *Picnic.*"

"I don't know who's on Marilyn's list of approved directors," Flack Jones said. "Under her original contract, she had no cast or script approval, and she doesn't now; but most of the time that really doesn't matter. Usually if a star doesn't like a story or a script, the studio won't try to force him or her to do the picture. It's only in rare cases, when the studio suspects that the star has other reasons up his sleeve (or down her bosom) that pressure is applied."

"Do her pictures make a lot of money?" I asked.

"*How to Marry a Millionaire* earned a tremendous amount," Jones said.

"What about *The Seven Year Itch?*" I asked.

"*Variety* says it was the top Fox grosser for 1955," he said.

"There's nothing in the way she's handled her affairs so far to indicate that she's stupid in any way. I was one of those who were convinced that she was going to come back to Fox someday, and that she would work out some sort of a compromise with the studio. It figured.

"Not that it necessarily followed," Flack Jones went on judicially. "There have been plenty of cases in this industry where a person has been so sharp they've washed themselves up for good. There are two ways of doing it. You can stay away from the screen so long you're forgotten; or you can become willful and not do what your studio wants you to do.

"I remember the girl half of the biggest boy-girl teams in the history of pictures. I won't give their names, but the girl wouldn't show up for work, so her studio put her on suspension. That ended her career. She could never pick it up again. Once you've pricked a popularity balloon something happens. I don't know exactly what it is. It can be one of several things. Somebody else fills the public's mind. People get interested in different personalities. Styles in personalities change.

"Making a success of being a screen personality is like putting on a successful play," he went on. "A play is successful or unsuccessful because of the audience's reaction to what's going on behind the footlights. It takes not only a player but an audience to make a play. The same is true of a personality. A personality without an audience runs the risk of not being a personality any more. They say that if a tree falls in a forest and there's nobody there to hear it, it makes no noise. A personality can wave at people from a hotel window, or even have Ed Murrow visit them on "Person to Person," but that's not the same as being on the screen. There comes a time when you've got to *re*-prove to the public that you're a screen personality, and if the people can't see you and hear your personality in a role, you're dead."

"Is there any way to tell how successful Marilyn's pictures would have been if she hadn't been in them and if some other girl had been in them instead?" I asked.

"The only answer I know to that," Flack Jones said, "is that we've had other girls in other pictures, but none of them have paid off the way Marilyn has paid off in her own particular type of thing. She's a girl who is phenomenally successful in what she does. She may be limited, she may not be wearing mentally, but she comes off beautifully."

"How long do you think she could have stayed away and still have retained her box-office appeal?" I asked him.

"She still had a big margin of safety when she signed her new contract," Flack Jones said. "Her publicity never stopped being sensational.

"It's going to be very interesting to see how her return to the screen turns out," Flack Jones said. "They'll get her next picture, *Bus Stop,* out as soon as possible. But even if they do, there'll be about a year and a half between the first showing of *Seven Year Itch* and the release of *Bus.* That's a long time to be off the screen. As a rule of thumb, in building a career, an actor or an actress ought to do from two to three pictures a year. This has proved out over a length of time.

"Of course, unusual personalities like Clark Gable or Bing Crosby, who've been established for many years, can do only an occasional picture and it's all right. They can coast. But you've got to have a terrifically strong backlog of work behind you to get away with that. Even Gable felt that he had to do two pictures in 1955 — *Soldier of Fortune* and *The Tall Men* — and he's a far more established star

112

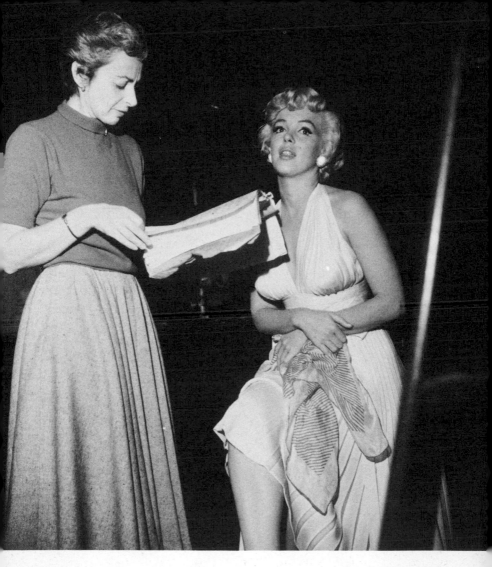

"Here's a girl who's built herself a career on overstating something, and now she's made up her mind to understate." The dedicated drama student with dramatic coach. GLOBE

Then there's the frightened Marilyn Monroe, the product of a broken home and a battered childhood — a girl who still can't believe that she's that girl on the screen they're making all the fuss about. HANS KNOPF-PIX

than Marilyn. In fact, it's questionable whether she'll ever attain his status, for Gable is one of the greatest motion-picture stars of all time."

"Right now, as of today, no matter what she thinks, Marilyn's great value is as a personality, not as an actress," Billy Wilder said. "If she sets out to be artistic and dedicated, and she carries it so far that she's willing to wear Sloppy-Joe sweaters and go without make-up and let her hair hang straight as a string; this is not what has made her great to date. I don't say that it's beyond the realm of possibility that she can establish herself as a straight dramatic actress — but it will be another career for her, a starting all over."

I asked Marilyn if she were worried about whether people would accept her as a new and different Marilyn Monroe as a result of her attendance at the Actors' Studio.

She answered, "It will be up to the public but I have to satisfy something inside of me, too. That doesn't mean that all of a sudden I'm going to play old-maid parts. No matter how much a person learns about being a better actress, a person isn't suddenly going to change and wear high-necked, long-sleeved dresses and dye her hair black."

I tried to adjust my mind to the idea of Marilyn appearing as an old maid. I couldn't make it.

"When you go around town in your ordinary, everyday make-up, hair-do, and clothing, do people recognize you as Marilyn Monroe?" I asked her.

"I usually go in disguise," she told me.

"How do you mean disguise?" I asked

"I mean dark glasses and a thing pulled over my hair, and no make-up," she said. "In spite of that, I've had people stop me and say, 'I know who you are.' And I tell them, 'Oh no, you're wrong. I'm Sheree North,' or 'I'm Mamie Van Doren.'

115

" 'Oh no you're not!' they tell me. 'We recognize the voice.' "

I said that I'd heard she'd spent sometime with Terence Rattigan, the British playwright, discussing the screen play he was adapting for her from his London stage success, *The Sleeping Prince,* a vehicle in which Sir Laurence Olivier played the prince. Sir Laurence had agreed to play the same role opposite Marilyn and to direct the film.

"I had a bad cold the evening I spent with Mr. Rattigan, and he said I sounded like Tallulah Bankhead," Marilyn told me proudly. She added thoughtfully, "Mr. Rattigan is young, but not too young."

I asked her what she meant by that. I said that millions of men would be interested in her reply. She smiled and said, "I guess you want me to say, 'Over twelve and not quite ninety.' Actually, I don't know how old Mr. Rattigan is. You might say he's kind of ageless." Rattigan is really forty-six.

I asked her if she'd mind giving me some hint of the story line followed by *The Sleeping Prince.* 'In it I'm an American chorus girl in London," she said; "the regent of a foreign country notices me and asks me to a reception at his country's legation. I wriggle into my only formal and go. It turns out it's not a large gathering at all. In fact, it's the same stale old bit that's been tried on girls for the last three thousand years; dinner for two, candles, wine and soft music, when she's expecting other guests. The next thing I know, I've had too much champagne and I've passed out. I won't tell you any more. You ought to be willing to spend your money to find out what happens next.

"The truth is," she said, "the plot is about a man who's been asleep — at least his emotional something or other has been asleep — but little by little a relationship builds up

116

Marilyn is to appear in a Terence Rattigan play-made-into-a-movie, and no less a person than Sir Laurence Olivier himself is going to appear in it with her and direct it — a teaming together described as "one of the least likely duos in cinematic history." This caused Milton Greene (left) to arrange a press conference. "Never have so many breathed so hard for so few — the male newsmen for Marilyn; the girl reporters for the handsome Sir Laurence." HANS KNOPF-PIX

She told me that she'd rather I wouldn't use a tape-recording machine while interviewing her. "It would make me nervous to see that thing going around and around," she insisted. HANS KNOPF-PIX

"... Grushenka is a sex pot ... Dostoevski knew what he was doing ... Marilyn knows what she is doing, too. She would be a good Grushenka." Cecil Beaton, the British photographer who usually shoots royalty, shoots a different queen.   HANS KNOPF-PIX

between him and this American chorus girl, and he begins to stir in his sleep, you might say. He's a married man, but that doesn't complicate things because he's sophisticated about the whole deal. Terence Rattigan describes it as 'an occasional fairy tale or a comedy with serious overtones.' "

As a proper "kick off" for the fact that not only was Marilyn to appear in the Terence Rattigan play-made-into-movie but that no less a person than Mister Fabulous — Sir Laurence Olivier himself — was going to appear in it with her and direct it — a teaming-together described by one of those present as "one of the least likely duos in cinematic history" — a press conference had been held in the Terrace Room of the Plaza Hotel in New York.

There were 150 reporters, photographers, television cameramen, and publicity workers on hand.

Of those 150 a reporter named Morris Goldberg of the New York *Enquirer* did the kind of bang-up, perceptive job every reporter dreams of doing (or talks of doing over his sixth beer at Bleeck's) but seldom does.

"Never have so many breathed so hard for so few — the male newsman for Marilyn — the girl reporters for the handsome Sir Laurence," Goldberg wrote afterward. "Marilyn wore a velvet sheath gown, a wisp of an Indian sari around her shoulders, and drop earrings of five small pearls connected with gold links. . . . Her neckline was so deep that when a photographer asked her to lean forward and she did so, he found time to blush and to beg her: 'Not too far, please.'

" 'Whisper in his ear!' another shouted, and Marilyn leaned toward Sir Laurence and whispered."

Goldberg asked Sir Laurence whether he agreed that as an actress, Marilyn had more sex appeal than any other woman in the world, and Sir Larry said that she had a "cunning way of suggesting naughtiness and innocence at the same time."

When Goldberg repeated the question because he didn't think it had been answered directly, Marilyn said in a small voice, "I don't think that's a fair question to ask Sir Laurence."

Goldberg made note of the fact that when another reporter asked, "Will you ask for police protection on location?" anticipating the crush that will follow a Monroe appearance in London, Sir Laurence looked at Marilyn and he said, "I believe we will." Then he repeated it: "I believe we will."

I'd also been lucky enough to have a good friend of mine on hand for that shindig; one of the greatest photographers in the U.S.A.; a small, effervescent dark, sentimental genius named Hans Knopf.

Hans relayed his experience to me. He speaks with certain European overtones and tricks of speech; not like Billy Wilder's, but still different from any Yankee argot I've ever heard.

"Marilyn was obviously tremendously happy and very gay and very pleased to appear with Laurence Olivier for this press conference," Hans told me. "Because he is such a great actor, she knew that to work with Sir Laurence would enhance her stature very much before the public. At that moment the opinion of the public about her was doubtful as far as her standing as a person and as an actress was concerned. By that I mean I think people were undecided as to whether she is good as an actress or not. They were determined to look at her as a piece of cheesecake. But being in the company of Sir Laurence Olivier could to a large degree destroy this point of view. I am sure that she thinks that some of his great skill will rub off on her. Not only will that be very good for her prestige; but secondly, her self-confidence has been greatly strengthened by the fact that Laurence Olivier seems to believe in her."

"Tell me how Laurence Olivier conducted himself at the press conference," I asked.

"They both appeared together, at the same time," Hans said. "Sir Laurence wore a dark suit, a white shirt, a dark tie; he was very elegantly and conservatively dressed. Marilyn had on a silk black dress, help up by two very thin straps. She at first came in with her shoulders covered by a black silken cape. Later she took it off and a great 'ah' and 'oh' filled the air because of her naked shoulders. This is what had been expected. Then Sir Laurence and Marilyn were photographed — which lasted, I would say, about twenty minutes — and while they were photographed they were being interviewed by a number of reporters, who were asking them questions. But to me, the interview really took place after the picture-taking ended. They were at this time sitting at another table at which there was a microphone. I would say that three quarters of the questions were fired at Marilyn.

"During this period it was most interesting to watch Sir Laurence. He took over the microphone and he repeated each question put to Marilyn, in a very slow, deliberate manner, looking into space, and evidently obviously trying to give her a chance to think her answers over very carefully. Very often he answered for her. You could see Marilyn very slowly growing in courage, thanks to Sir Laurence's handling of the conference, and she put in a few nice answers herself."

"How did Sir Larry like that?" I asked, remembering another press conference in Tokyo and a man named DiMaggio who'd been present but who'd been largely ignored.

"The questions Sir Laurence was asked were very blunt," Hans said. "For example, he was asked what he thought of her as an actress, which obviously in front of Marilyn was a difficult question to answer. But he answered all these difficult questions in a manner which a superior statesman like Sir Anthony Eden couldn't have surpassed. He managed to wear the air of an aristocrat and a diplomat at the same time, which is not easy to do.

"He gave a terrific performance as a gentleman and protector of sweet womanhood," Hans concluded. "He didn't seem to be annoyed. He was most fair and most patient. He apparently knew all about the habits of the American press, so he was by no means intimidated by the most brutal questions.

"The conference ended, I think, with the reporters running out of questions.

"One question put to Marilyn was did she still want to play *The Brothers Karamazov*," Hans added. She said, 'I never intended to play *The Brothers Karamazov*. I want to play the girl Grushenka in *The Brothers Karamazov*.' Another reporter asked her nastily, 'How do you spell Grushenka?' thinking that he had trapped her and that she was too stupid to know. And she, with a very superior smile and a twinkle in her eyes, said, 'You can look it up in the book,' which was proof that Sir Laurence had given her courage by being there. At that the reporters laughed and their questions were less sarcastic, less loaded, less angled to make a patsy — a fall girl — of her."

Putting that press conference out of my mind, I turned to Billy Wilder on my left and said, "I should think it would take a great deal of mature mental and moral strength to cope with becoming an enormous success overnight. It must be unsettling to suddenly become a sex symbol known all over the world.

"It's my opinion that she's basically a good girl," Wilder replied, "but what's happened to her is enough to drive almost anybody slightly daffy, even someone whose background has armored her with poise and calmness. But you take a girl like Marilyn, who's never really had a chance to learn, who's never really had a chance to live, and you suddenly confront her with a Frankenstein's monster of herself built of fame and publicity and notoriety, and naturally she's a little mixed up and made giddy by it all.

"Anyhow I'd like to go on record with this: I worked with her in *Seven Year Itch* and I had a good time with her. She was seldom on time, but it wasn't because she overslept. It was because she had to force herself to come to the studio. She's emotionally upset all the time; she's scared and unsure of herself — so much so that when I worked with her I found myself wishing that I were a psychoanalyst and she were my patient." He grinned. "It might be that I couldn't have helped her, but she would have looked lovely on a couch."

"You mean you didn't get annoyed when she was late?" I asked.

"I understood the reasons for it," Wilder told me. "There was no use getting annoyed. Even at the beginning, when I discovered that I had let myself in for a certain amount of trouble, I found myself liking her. At no time did I find her malicious, mean, capricious, or anything but conscientious. There are certain urges and drives in her which make her different, but as a director, I think it worth putting up with those things and diving with them in order to work with her."

123

It seemed a good time to saw off the bull session I had conjured up by snapping my fingers.

I snapped my fingers again.

There was no more Loggia, or pepper tree, or pink napery or Rhubarb the cat or white wrought-iron tables and chairs. Marilyn and Milton H. Greene and Wilder and Flack Jones were gone.

I was back once more in Marilyn's apartment on Sutton Place South in New York, trying to wrap up the loose ends of my series of Marilyn Monroe interviews. I had two more questions I wanted to ask her. I was curious about how she thought the public would feel about her as a dedicated actress with a capital *A;* and whether or not she was worried about her ability to turn in a convincing as well as moving performance in the movie version of *Bus Stop.*

I found myself hoping that Josh Logan, who will direct her in the filmed version of *Bus Stop,* and Buddy Adler, who bought that play for Fox and who will produce it, would feel the same way about her that Wilder feels.

She does that to you. In spite of her spells of proscrastination carried to fantastic lengths, and in spite of her sometimes shallow perceptions, you wind up liking her.

By "her" I mean *all* of the various Marilyn Monroes — and there are several of them. There is the sex-pot Marilyn Monroe; the one who tries so hard to live up to the legend of her sexiness that her stomach sometimes can't take it. Then there's the frightened Marilyn Monroe, the product of a broken home and a battered childhood — a girl named Mortenson who still can't believe that she's that girl on the screen they're making all the fuss about. And last, there's "The New Marilyn Monroe" — the one who's supposed to

124

have emerged from the Actors' studio a composed and studied performer, having, as she puts it, "achieved growth" and "developed more."

I wondered.

A pair of very bright young men — the kind who once (but no longer) made the Gray Flannel Suit a uniform without which all *Time, Life,* and Madison Avenue former Ivy Leaguers felt themselves in mufti — ran up a few notes about Marilyn back in April 1952. One of the twain was Stan Flink, now an associate producer for NBC on the Dave Garroway show. The other was the equally talented Robert Wernick.

As those notes appeared in *Life,* the publication for which they worked, their words came out like this:

"Because her movie role is always that of a dumb blonde, Hollywood generally supposes she is pretty dumb herself. This is a delusion. Marilyn is naïve and guileless. But she is smart enough to have known how to make a success in the cutthroat world of glamor. She does it by being as wholly natural as the world will allow. Physically she has many of the attributes of Jean Harlow. But there is no suggestion of hardness or tartness in Marilyn. She is relaxed, warm, apparently absorbed by whatever man she has her big blue eyes fixed on at any particular moment.

"Marilyn looks back on the hard knocks of her youth with no particular self-pity and only hopes they may have taught her a few things about people which will help her in her career. For, with all Hollywood at her feet, she is obsessed by an irrational childhood ambition: she wants very much to become an actress."

Those two young men who labored in the Luce salt mines wrought well. In some manner they contrived to be discerning, aware, sensitive to human nuances, and capable of seeing behind a façade — although, as façades go, Marilyn's is pretty distracting — in their summing up of the former Mrs. Dougherty, nee Mortensen, for it still holds true as a clue to what she's all about.

One of the most knowledgeable men about Hollywood and its workings I know is Nunnally Johnson. He is wise, kind, and more than a hit-or-miss judge of matters Monroe, having worked with her in the movie *How to Marry a Millionaire* — as hereinfore recorded. However, it should be noted that the following comments about Marilyn were made by Johnson *before* she was shown the light by the Actors' Studio.

"Speaking for myself, I can't say that I saw a 'new Marilyn Monroe,' in *The Seven Year Itch,* that some others did," he told me. "I thought that essentially it was the same performance, just longer. Still, this could scarcely be a cause for worry for her; God had given her that equipment and it was still magnificent. She was still a phenomenon."

"Maybe she'll grow into a young Mae West and make people laugh at sex," I suggested.

Johnson agreed that it might be a good thing if she could do that. "I believe that the first time anybody genuinely liked Marilyn for herself, in a picture, was in *How to Marry a Millionaire,*" he said. "She herself diagnosed the reason for that very shrewdly, I think. She said that this was the only picture she'd been in in which she had a measure of modesty. Not physical modesty, but modesty about her own attractiveness. In *Millionaire* she was nearsighted; she didn't think men would look at her twice because she wore glasses; she blundered into walls and stumbled into things and she was most disarming. In the course of the plot she married an astigmatic; so there they were, a couple of astigmatic lovers. In her other pictures they've cast her as a somewhat arrogant sex trap, but when *Millionaire* was

126

released, I heard people say, 'Why, I really liked her!' in surprised tones."

(However, upon her return from New York to work on the Fox lot in *Bus Stop,* Johnson wrote me that he *did* see a "new Marilyn Monroe."

"In contrast to the old Marilyn, in her present incarnation she is a liberated soul, happy, co-operative, friendly, relaxed," he reported. "Actually, it is as if she had undergone a psychoanalysis so successful that the analyst himself was flabbergasted. Now she's different; her behavior and her manner as a member of the social order are O.K. As for her acting; that remains to be seen.")

But somehow, I found myself hoping that people would accept her as the new and different Marilyn Monroe she thinks she is. I had heard one man say, "Even if you hung Ethel Barrymore's and Helen Hayes' talent on Marilyn's beautiful body, people wouldn't take her acting seriously." And to my surprise, I realized that I was dreading the possibility that when she turned on her new brand of acting, audiences might laugh at her, as they laughed at Zasu Pitts when she went in for "heavy drama" after a lifetime spent as a comedienne.

When I mentioned my fears of Marilyn, she told me bravely, "It doesn't scare me. If I have the same things I had before I started to go to the Actors' Studio and I've added more — well, how can I lose?"

I tried to find out if she was worried about her ability to do as well on the screen in *Bus Stop* as Kim Stanley had done on Broadway in the same role. And Marilyn said, "It doesn't bother me in the least. It'll be two different characterizations by two different people, and I'm looking forward to it. Maybe I feel this way because I've gotten older inside. Remember, I said inside. Not outside. I'd like to think of my life as having started right now. Somebody asked me when I was born and I said, 'Just recently, in New York.'"

Whether that is true or not, I don't know. But, as she herself points out, she does — emphatically — still have the same things she had before. My guess is that they're still negotiable at the box office.